D. HEALY

ORIGAMI
U ★ S ★ A

Duy Nguyen

Sterling Publishing Co., Inc.
New York

Design by Judy Morgan
Edited by Claire Bazinet

Library of Congress Cataloging-in-Publication Data
Nguyen, Duy, 1960-
  Origami USA / Duy Nguyen.
      p. cm.
  ISBN 1-4027-0928-5
  1. Origami. I. Title.
TT870 .N488 2003
736'982--dc22

                    2003019712

10 9 8 7 6 5 4 3 2 1

Published by Sterling Publishing Co., Inc.
387 Park Avenue South, New York, NY 10016
© 2004 by Duy Nguyen
Distributed in Canada by Sterling Publishing
℅ Canadian Manda Group, One Atlantic Avenue, Suite 105
Toronto, Ontario, Canada M6K 3E7
Distributed in Great Britain and Europe by Chris Lloyd at Orca Book
Services, Stanley House, Fleets Lane, Poole BH15 3AJ, England
Distributed in Australia by Capricorn Link (Australia) Pty. Ltd.
P.O. Box 704, Windsor, NSW 2756, Australia
Printed in China

Sterling ISBN 1-4027-0928-5

Contents

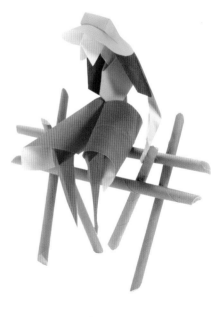

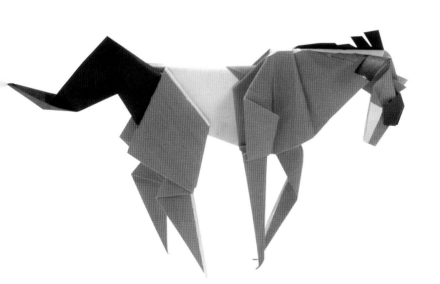

Preface

A word of encouragement. When I first began learning origami, I struggled with even the simplest folds. I would look back at the instructions at the beginning of the book again and again, reviewing the basic folds. I also looked ahead, at the diagram showing the next step of whatever project I was folding, to see how it *should* look, to be certain I was following the instructions correctly. Looking ahead at the "next step," the result of a fold, is incidentally a very good way for a beginner to learn origami.

Another way to make learning origami easier is to create "construction lines" before doing a complex fold. By this I mean to pre-fold and unfold, creasing the form to create guidelines. When preparing to fold a pleat fold reverse or an inside or outside reverse fold, for example, if you pre-crease, using mountain and valley folds, the finished fold is more likely to match the one shown in the book. Folds that look different, because of slightly different angles, can "throw you off."

These learning techniques, and others you will quickly pick up as you do the original forms in this book, will soon have you crafting and leaving a paper trail of figures…in the USA, or wherever you are in the world.

Duy Nguyen

Basic Instructions

Paper: The best paper to use for origami is thin, keeps a crease well, and folds flat. You can use plain white paper, solid-color paper, or wrapping paper. Be aware, though, that some papers stretch slightly in length or width, while others tear easily. Printing off one-sided colored sheets and squaring them off (see page 5) will work fine with these projects. Scraps can be used for accessories and other trims, or to simply add a layer of color to parts of a figure. Packets of origami paper (15 and 21 cm square, about 6 and 8 in) are widely available in a variety of colors.

Typing or copying paper may be too heavy for the many tight folds needed in complex, traditional origami figures, but it should be fine for larger papercraft works with fewer folds. For those who are learning or have a problem getting their fingers to work tight folds, larger paper sizes are also fine. Certainly, slightly larger figures are easier to make than overly small ones.

Glue: Use an easy-flowing but not loose paper glue. Use it sparingly; don't soak the paper. A flat toothpick makes a good applicator. Allow the glued form time to dry. Avoid using stick glue, as the application pressure needed (especially if the stick has become dry) can damage your figure.

Technique: Fold with care. Position the paper, especially at corners, precisely and line edges up before creasing. Once you are sure of the fold, use a fingernail to make a clean, flat crease. Don't get discouraged with your first efforts. In time, what your mind can create, your fingers can fashion.

Symbols & Lines

Fold lines	valley		Fold then unfold	← →
	mountain	— · — · — · —		
Cut line		+++++++++++++	Pleat fold (repeated folding)	
Turn over or rotate			Crease line	—

Squaring-Off Paper

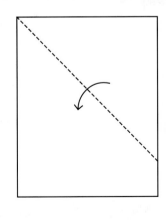

1
Take a rectangular sheet of paper and valley fold it diagonally to opposite edge.

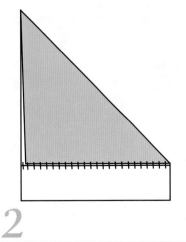

2
Cut off excess on long side as shown.

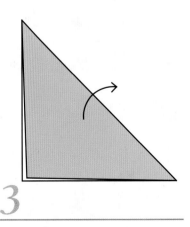

3
Unfold, and sheet is square.

Basic Folds

Kite Fold

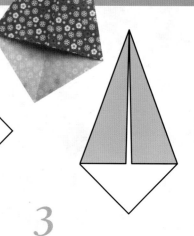

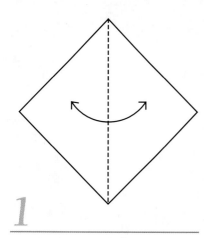

1

Fold and unfold a square diagonally, making a center crease.

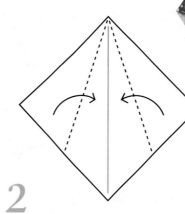

2

Fold both sides in to the center crease.

3

This is a kite form.

Valley Fold   - - - - - - - - - - - - - - - - -

1

Here, using the kite, fold form toward you (forward), making a "valley."

2

This fold forward is a valley fold.

Mountain Fold   - · - · - · - · - · - · - ·

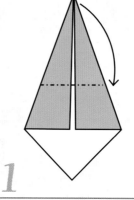

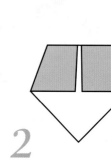

1

Here, using the kite, fold form away from you (backwards), making a "mountain."

2

This fold backwards is a mountain fold.

Inside Reverse Fold

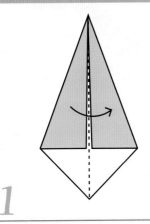

1
Starting here with a kite, valley fold kite closed.

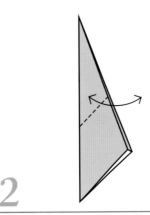

2
Valley fold as marked to crease, then unfold.

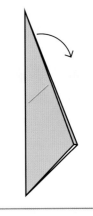

3
Pull tip in direction of arrow.

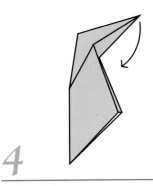

4
Appearance before completion.

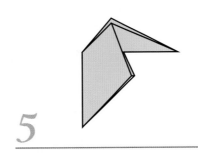

5
You've made an inside reverse fold.

Outside Reverse Fold

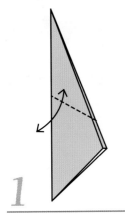

1
Using closed kite, valley fold, unfold.

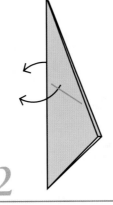

2
Fold inside out, as shown by arrows.

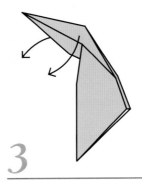

3
Appearance before completion.

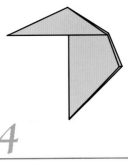

4
You've made an outside reverse fold.

Pleat Fold

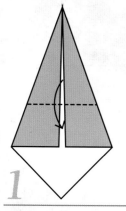 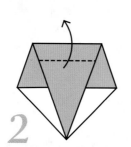 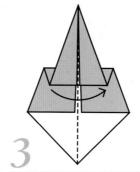 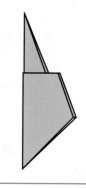

1	*2*	*3*	*4*
Here, using the kite, valley fold.	Valley fold back again.	This is a pleat. Valley fold in half.	You've made a pleat fold.

Pleat Fold Reverse

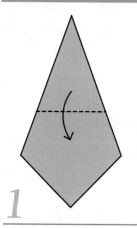 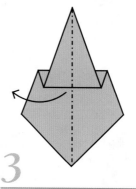 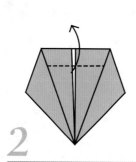 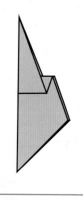

1	*2*	*3*	*4*
Here, using the kite form backwards, valley fold.	Valley fold back again for pleat.	Mountain fold form in half.	This is a pleat fold reverse.

Squash Fold I

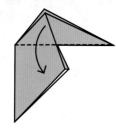 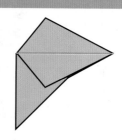

1	*2*
Using inside reverse, valley fold one side.	This is a squash fold I.

Squash Fold II

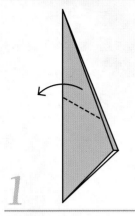

1 Using closed kite form, valley fold.

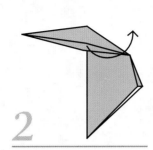

2 Open in direction of the arrow.

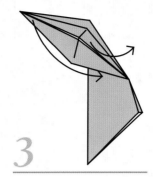

3 Appearance before completion.

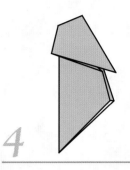

4 You've made a squash fold II.

Inside Crimp Fold

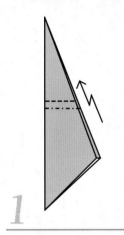

1 Here using closed kite form, pleat fold.

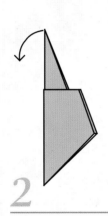

2 Pull tip in direction of the arrow.

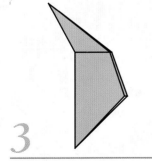

3 This is an inside crimp fold.

Outside Crimp Fold

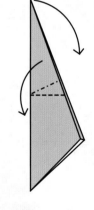

1 Here using closed kite form, pleat fold and unfold.

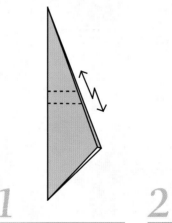

2 Fold mountain and valley as shown, both sides.

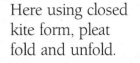

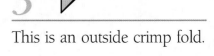

3 This is an outside crimp fold.

Basic Folds

Base Folds

Base folds are basic forms that do not in themselves produce origami, but serve as a basis, or jumping-off point, for a number of creative origami figures, some quite complex. As when beginning other crafts, learning to fold these base folds is not the most exciting part of origami. They are, however, easy to do, and will help you with your technique. They also quickly become rote, so much so that you can do many using different-colored papers while you are watching television or your mind is elsewhere. With completed base folds handy, if you want to quickly work up a form or are suddenly inspired with an idea for an original, unique figure, you can select an appropriate base fold and swiftly bring a new creation to life.

Base Fold I

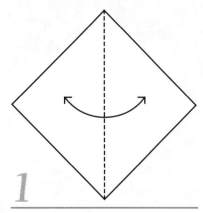

1
Fold and unfold in direction of arrow.

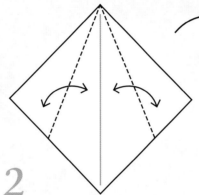

2
Fold both sides in to center crease, then unfold. Rotate.

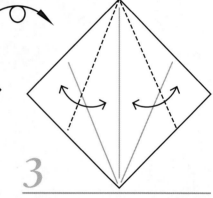

3
Fold both sides in to center crease, then unfold.

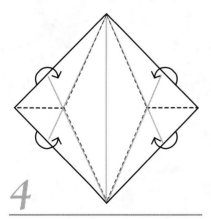

4
Pinch corners of square together and fold inward.

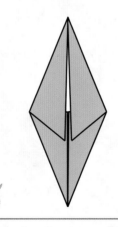

5
Completed Base Fold I.

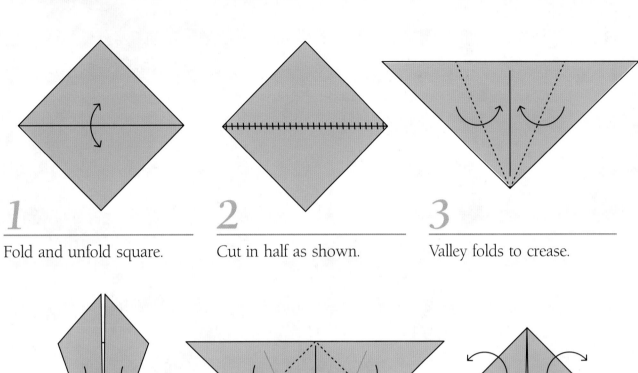

1 Fold and unfold square.

2 Cut in half as shown.

3 Valley folds to crease.

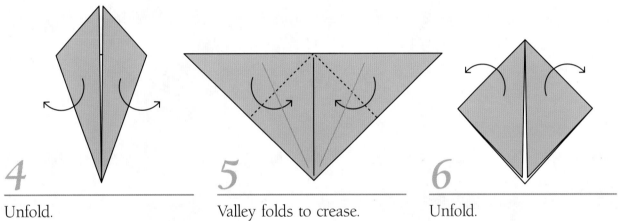

4 Unfold.

5 Valley folds to crease.

6 Unfold.

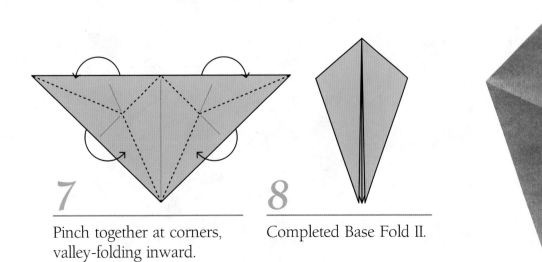

7 Pinch together at corners, valley-folding inward.

8 Completed Base Fold II.

Base Folds

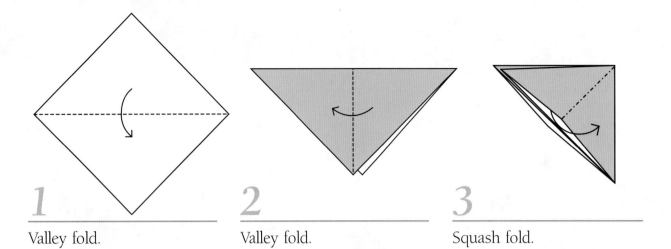

1

Valley fold.

2

Valley fold.

3

Squash fold.

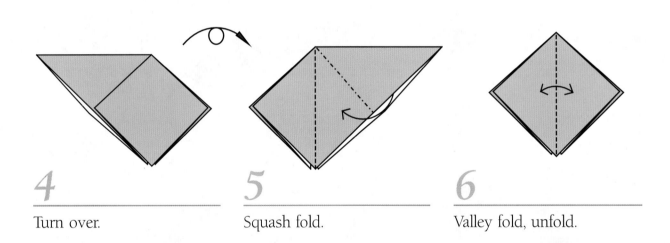

4

Turn over.

5

Squash fold.

6

Valley fold, unfold.

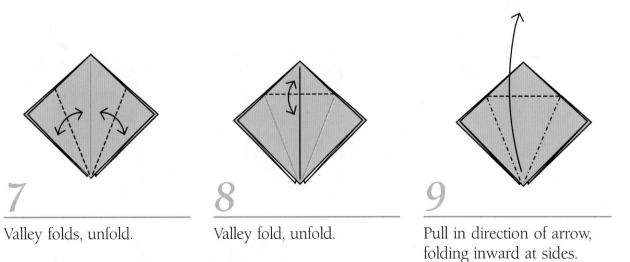

7

Valley folds, unfold.

8

Valley fold, unfold.

9

Pull in direction of arrow, folding inward at sides.

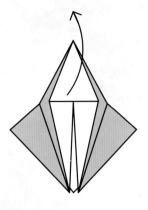

10

Appearance before
completion of fold.

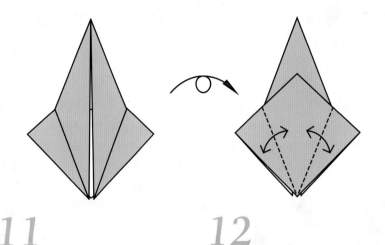

11

Fold completed. Turn over.

12

Valley folds, unfold.

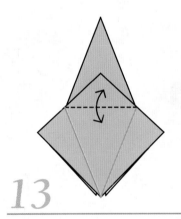

13

Valley fold, unfold.

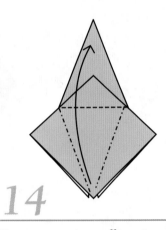

14

Repeat, again pulling in
direction of arrow.

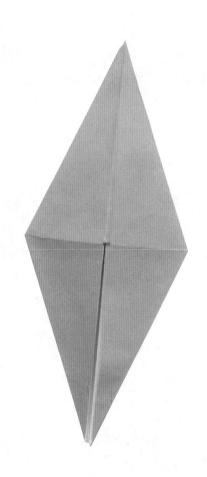

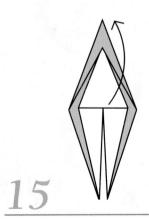

15

Appearance before
completion.

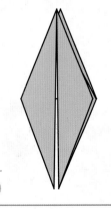

16

Completed Base Fold III.

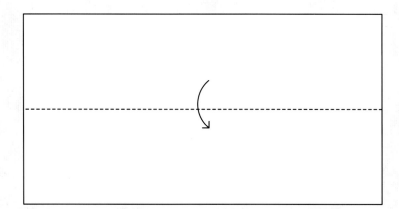

1

Valley fold rectangular size paper (length variable) in half as shown.

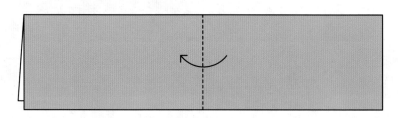

2

Valley fold in direction of arrow.

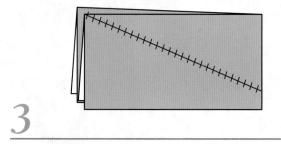

3

Make cut as shown.

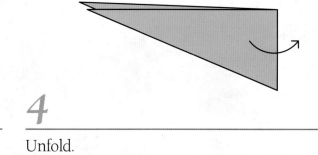

4

Unfold.

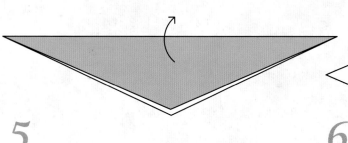

5

Unfold.

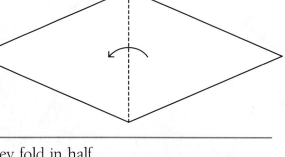

6

Valley fold in half.

Base Folds

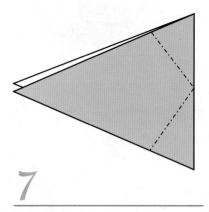

7

Inside reverse folds to inner center crease.

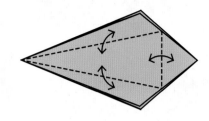

8

Valley fold and unfold to crease.

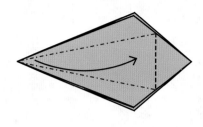

9

Pull in direction of arrow, and fold.

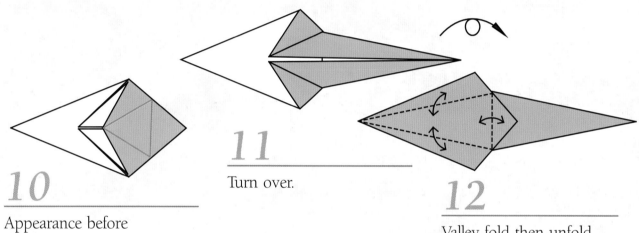

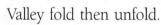

10

Appearance before completion.

11

Turn over.

12

Valley fold then unfold.

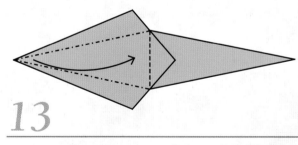

13

Again, pull in direction of arrow, and fold.

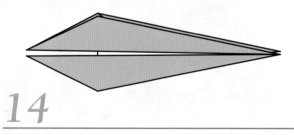

14

Completed Base Fold IV.

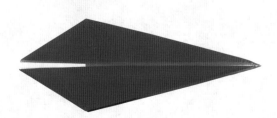

American Eagle

Part 1

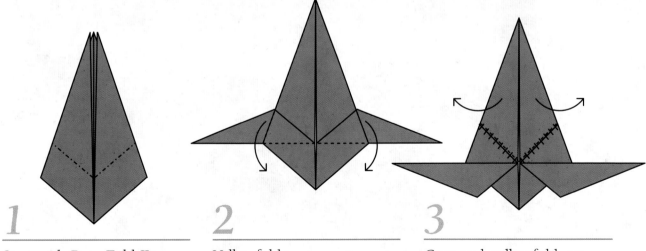

1
Start with Base Fold II.
Mountain folds.

2
Valley folds.

3
Cuts and valley fold cut
parts.

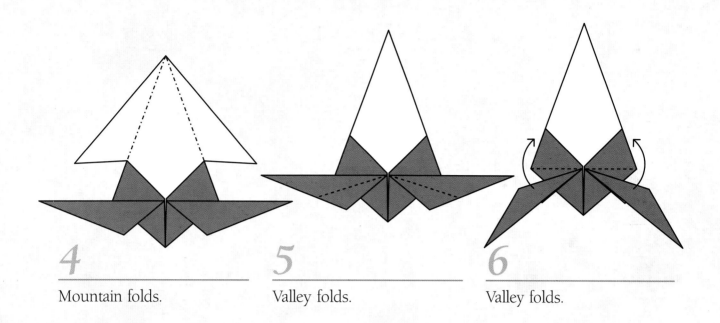

4

Mountain folds.

5

Valley folds.

6

Valley folds.

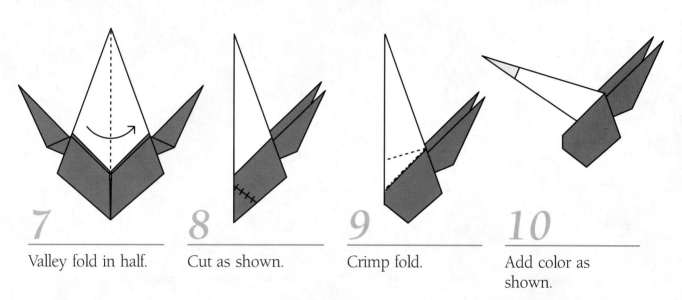

7

Valley fold in half.

8

Cut as shown.

9

Crimp fold.

10

Add color as shown.

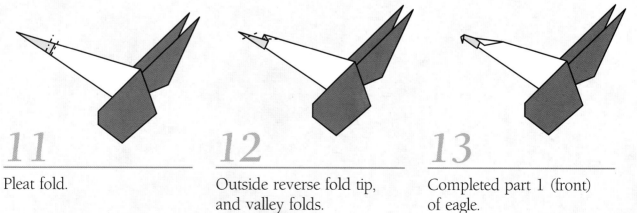

11

Pleat fold.

12

Outside reverse fold tip, and valley folds.

13

Completed part 1 (front) of eagle.

American Eagle

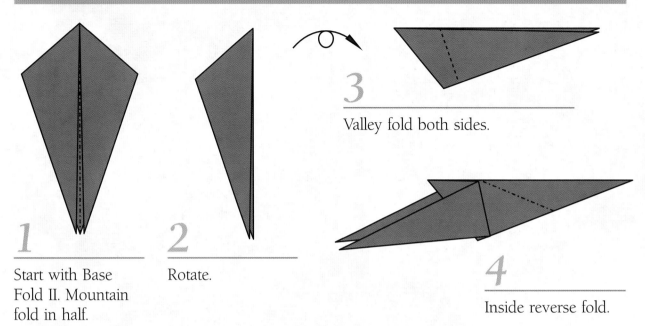

3

Valley fold both sides.

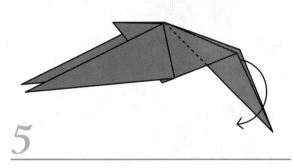

1

Start with Base
Fold II. Mountain
fold in half.

2

Rotate.

4

Inside reverse fold.

5

Valley fold both sides.

6

Cuts and valley fold both sides.

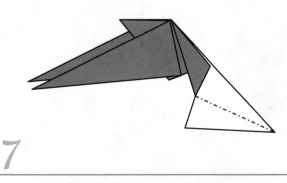

7

Mountain fold both front and back.

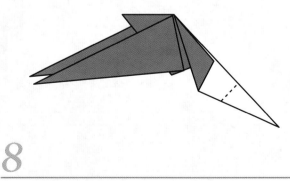

8

Inside reverse fold.

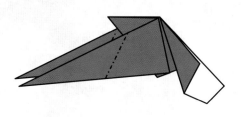

9

Mountain fold both sides.

10

Cut through on both sides.

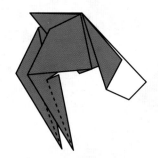

11

Valley fold all sides.

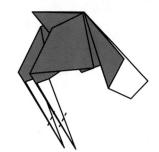

12

Outside reverse folds.

13

Repeat.

14

Outside reverse folds again.

15

Completed part 2 (rear) of eagle.

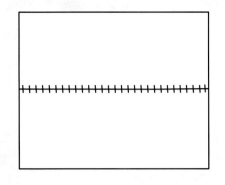

1

Cut sheet (8½ by 11 proportion) in half.

2

Valley fold half section.

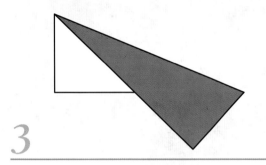

3

Completed wing.

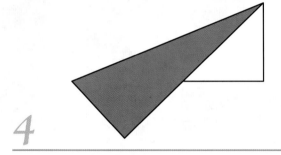

4

Using other half, repeat fold and rotate for another completed wing.

To Attach

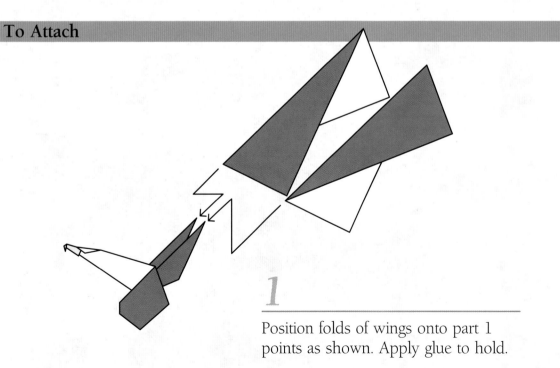

1

Position folds of wings onto part 1 points as shown. Apply glue to hold.

American Eagle

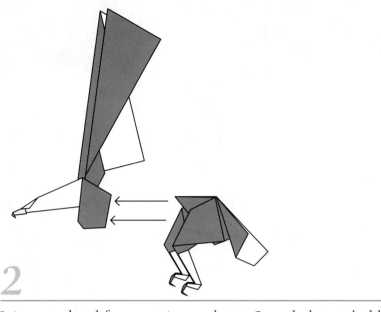

2

Join completed front section and part 2, and glue to hold.

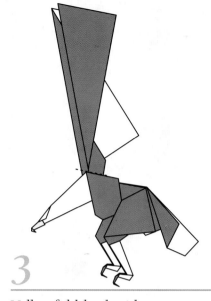

3

Valley fold both sides.

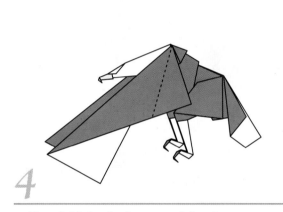

4

Valley fold both front and back.

5

Valley fold both front and back.

6

Stretch out (unfold) wings to completion.

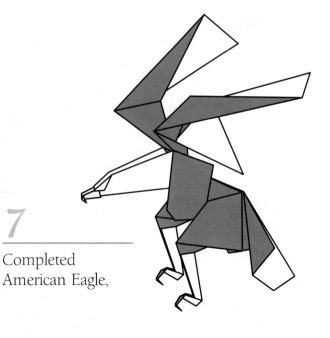

7

Completed American Eagle,

American Eagle

Part 4 (salmon)

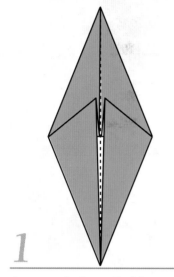

1

Start with Base Fold I.
Mountain fold in half.

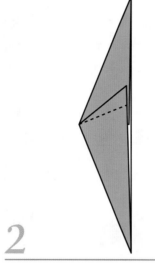

2

Valley folds.

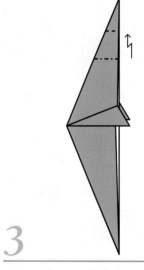

3

Open form slightly, and pleat
fold reverse.

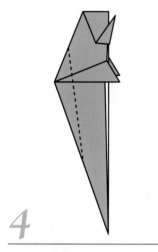

4

Valley folds.

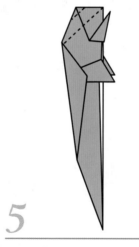

5

Pleat folds.

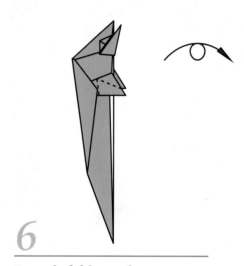

6

Squash folds, and rotate.

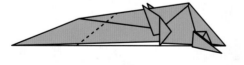

7

Outside reverse folds.

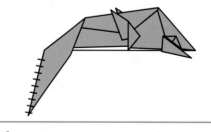

8

Cut as shown.

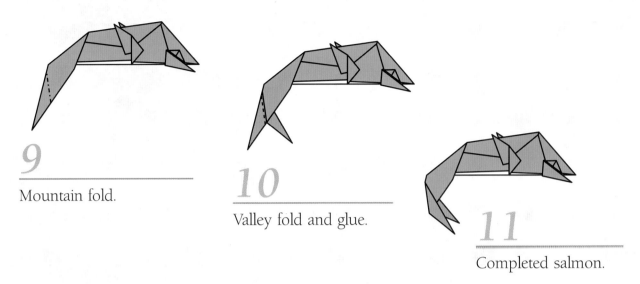

9
Mountain fold.

10
Valley fold and glue.

11
Completed salmon.

To Attach

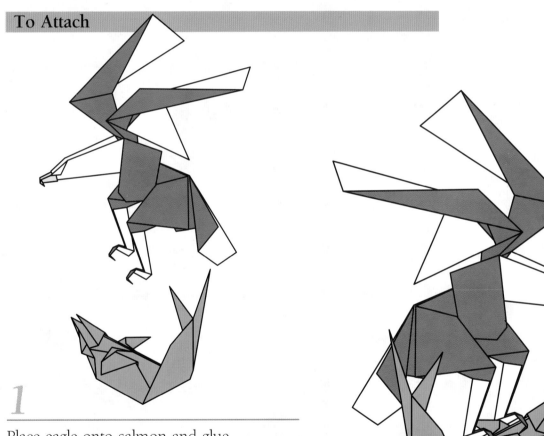

1
Place eagle onto salmon and glue.

2
Completed American Eagle (with catch).

American Eagle

Western Mustang

Part 1

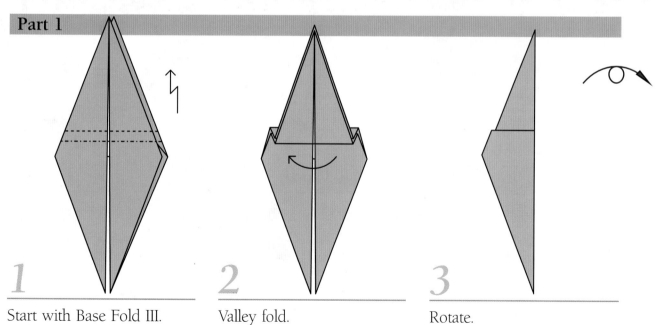

1
Start with Base Fold III.
Pleat fold through all layers.

2
Valley fold.

3
Rotate.

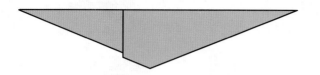

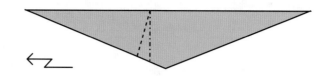

4

Unfold.

5

Crimp fold.

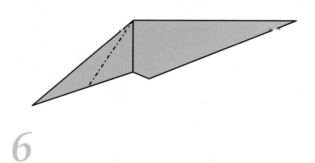

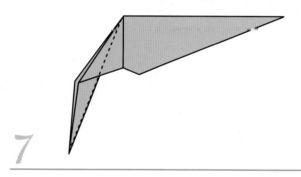

6

Inside reverse fold.

7

Valley fold.

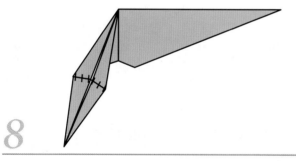

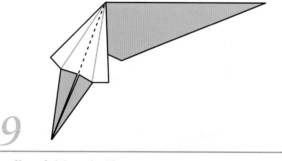

8

Cuts, then valley open.

9

Valley fold in half.

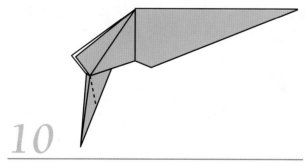

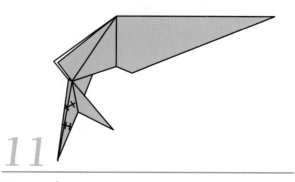

10

Outside reverse fold.

11

Cut as shown.

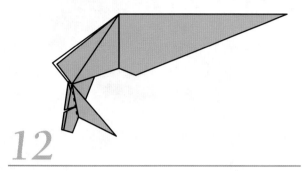

12

Valley folds, then outside reverse fold.

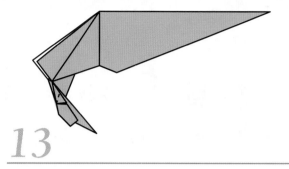

13

Valley folds.

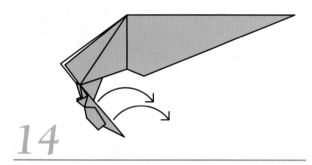

14

Pull some paper out.

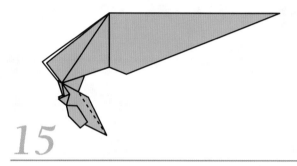

15

Valley folds.

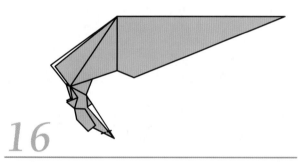

16

Inside reverse fold.

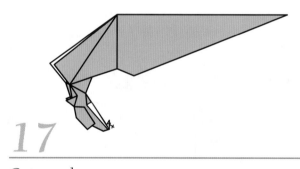

17

Cuts as shown.

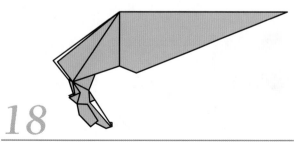

18

Hide ears between the head's layer.

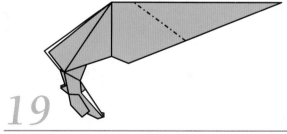

19

Inside reverse fold.

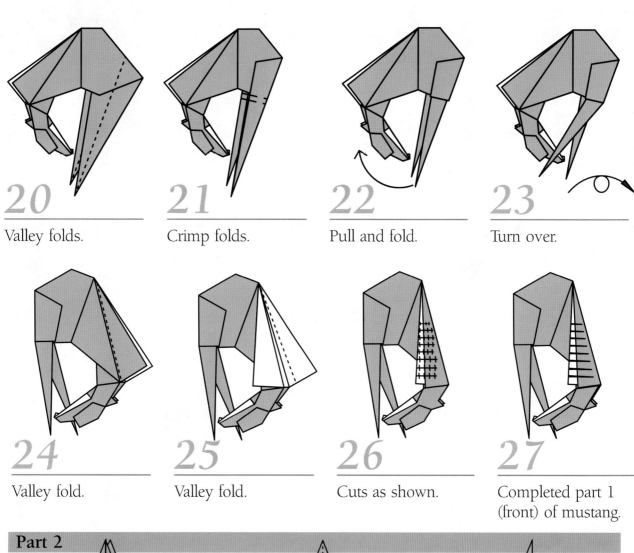

20 Valley folds.

21 Crimp folds.

22 Pull and fold.

23 Turn over.

24 Valley fold.

25 Valley fold.

26 Cuts as shown.

27 Completed part 1 (front) of mustang.

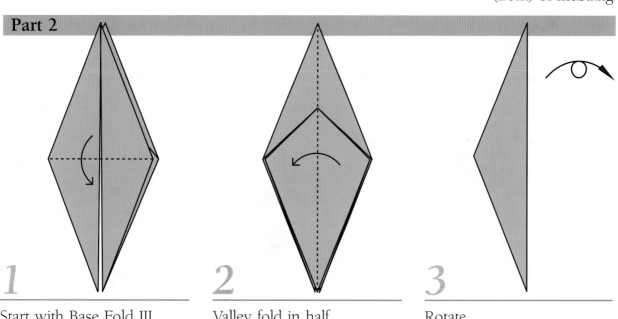

Part 2

1 Start with Base Fold III, then valley fold.

2 Valley fold in half.

3 Rotate.

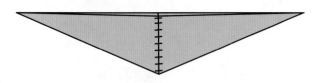

4

Cut top layer only, as shown.

5

Open in direction of arrow.

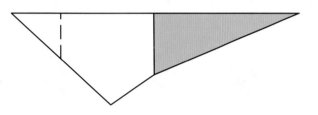

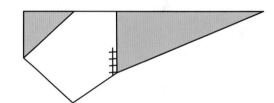

6

Outside reverse fold.

7

Cuts as shown.

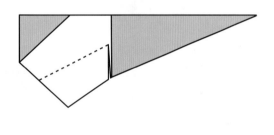

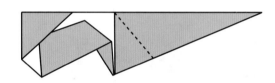

8

Valley fold.

9

Valley folds.

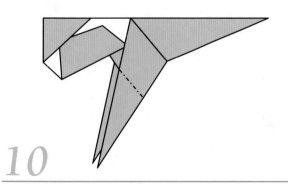

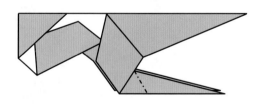

10

Inside reverse folds.

11

Inside reverse folds.

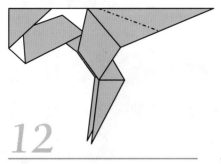

12

Inside reverse fold.

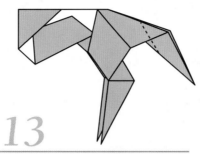

13

Outside reverse fold.

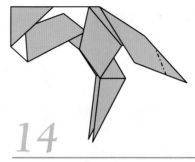

14

Inside reverse fold.

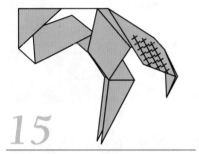

15

Cuts as shown.

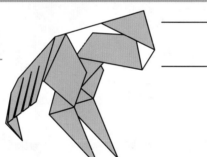

16

Pull, crimp into position.

17

Completed part 2 (rear) of mustang.

To Attach

1

Attach parts together as shown and apply glue to hold.

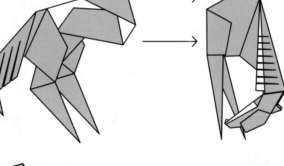
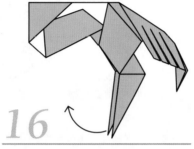

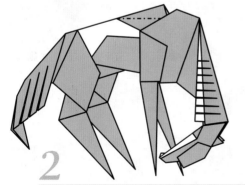

2

Inside reverse fold.

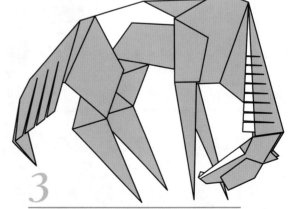

3

Completed Western Mustang.

Native American

Part 1

1	**2**	**3**	**4**
Start with Base Fold II. Valley folds.	Cuts, then valley folds back up.	Reverse fold sides.	Mountain folds.

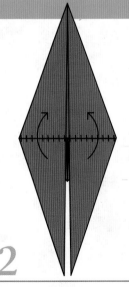
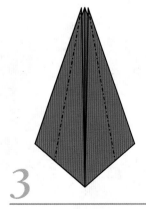

30

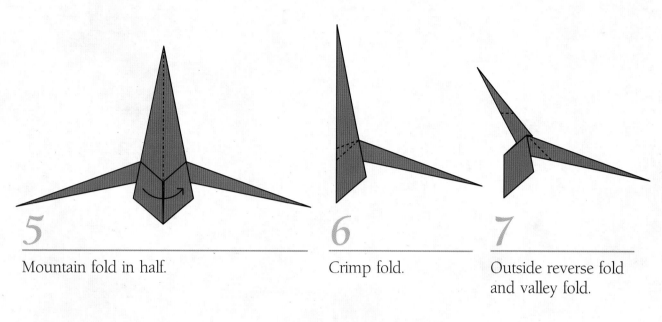

5
Mountain fold in half.

6
Crimp fold.

7
Outside reverse fold and valley fold.

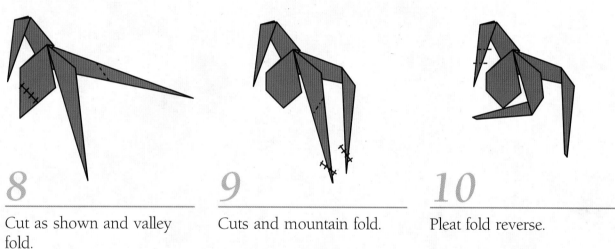

8
Cut as shown and valley fold.

9
Cuts and mountain fold.

10
Pleat fold reverse.

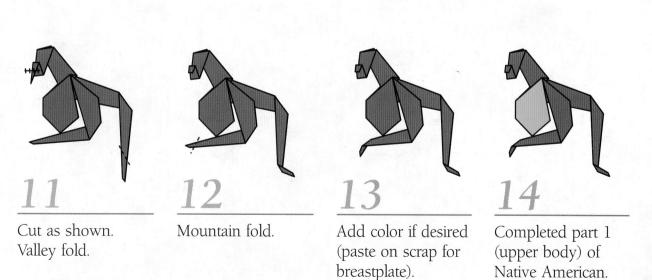

11
Cut as shown. Valley fold.

12
Mountain fold.

13
Add color if desired (paste on scrap for breastplate).

14
Completed part 1 (upper body) of Native American.

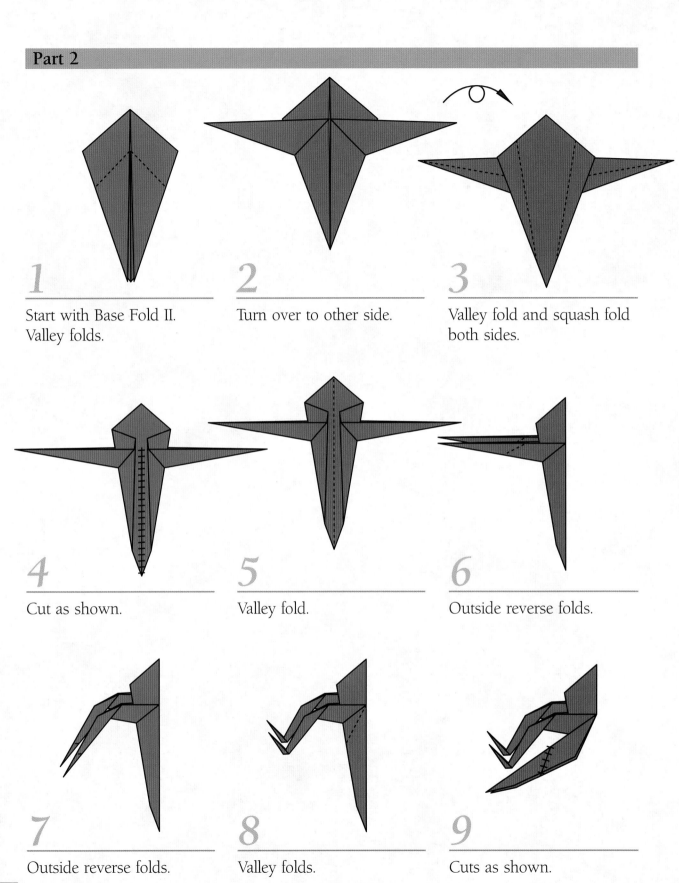

1

Start with Base Fold II.
Valley folds.

2

Turn over to other side.

3

Valley fold and squash fold
both sides.

4

Cut as shown.

5

Valley fold.

6

Outside reverse folds.

7

Outside reverse folds.

8

Valley folds.

9

Cuts as shown.

Native American

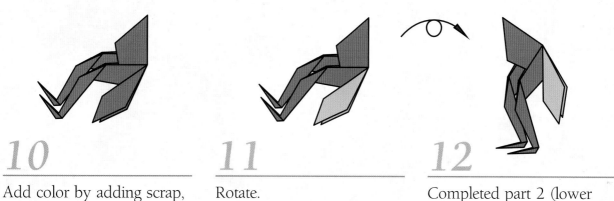

10

Add color by adding scrap, as before.

11

Rotate.

12

Completed part 2 (lower body) of Native American.

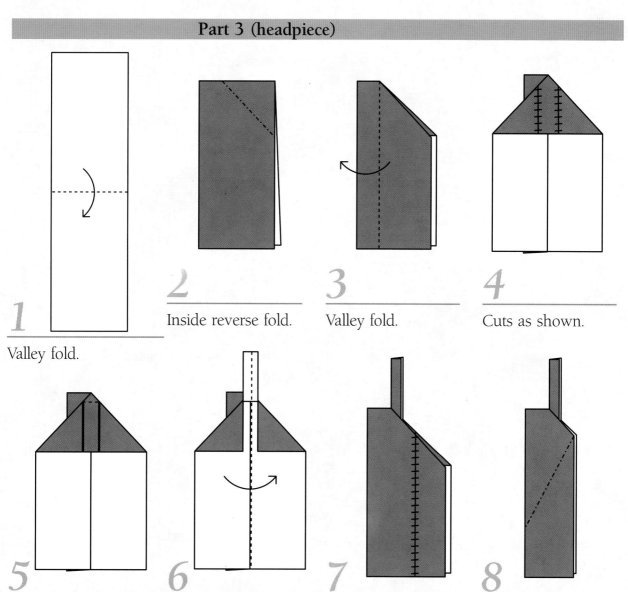

Part 3 (headpiece)

1

Valley fold.

2

Inside reverse fold.

3

Valley fold.

4

Cuts as shown.

5

Valley fold.

6

Valley fold.

7

Cut as shown.

8

Mountain folds.

Native American

33

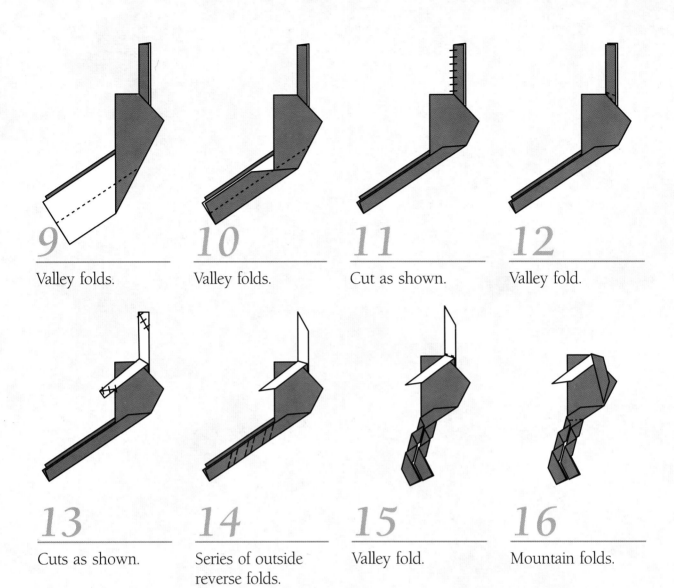

9

Valley folds.

10

Valley folds.

11

Cut as shown.

12

Valley fold.

13

Cuts as shown.

14

Series of outside
reverse folds.

15

Valley fold.

16

Mountain folds.

17

Completed part
3 (headpiece).

Part 4 (spear)

2

Make cuts and outside reverse folds.

1

Roll a square, corner to corner, into
a tight tube, and apply glue to hold.

3

Completed part 4 (spear).

Part 5 (shield)

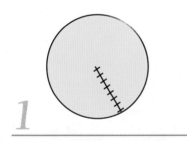

1

Cut circular piece as shown.

2

Valley fold thin strip of different color as shown.

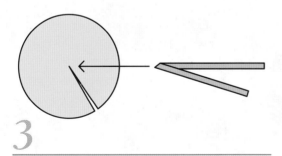

3

Position strip into opening, and apply
glue to hold.

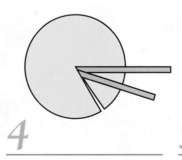

4

Pull shield and glue
into position.

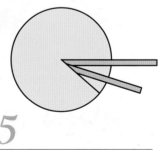

5

Completed part 5
(shield).

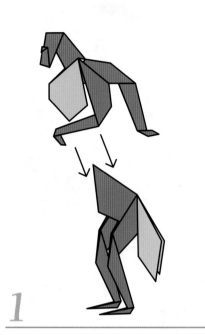

1

Join body parts and apply glue to hold.

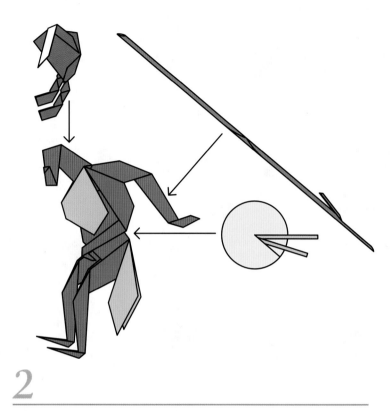

2

Glue on headpiece, spear, and shield.

3

Mountain fold to move spear into position.

4

Completed Native American.

Native American

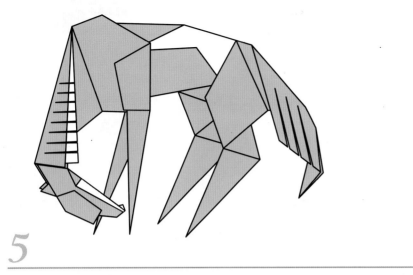

If wanted, position figure on mustang and apply glue to hold.

6

Completed and mounted Native American.

Buffalo

Part 1

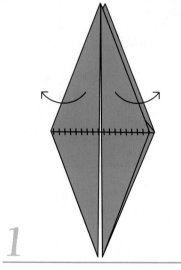

1

Start with Base Fold III. Cut top layer and valley unfold.

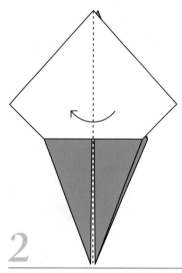

2

Valley fold in half.

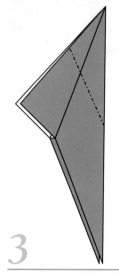

3

Inside reverse fold.

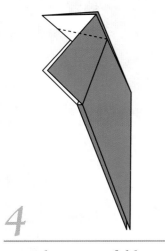

4

Outside reverse fold.

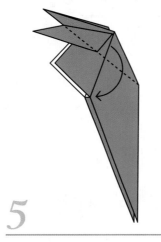

5

Valley fold.

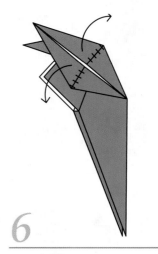

6

Cuts and valley unfold.

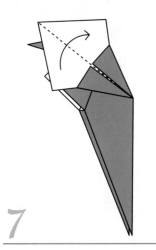

7

Valley fold.

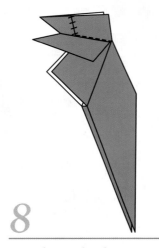

8

Cut through, then mountain folds to inside.

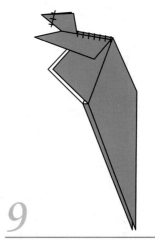

9

Cuts as shown.

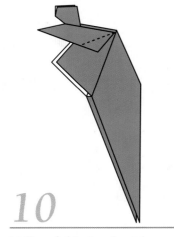

10

Valley folds both sides.

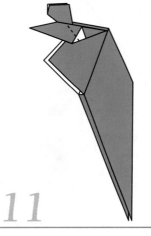

11

Valley folds again.

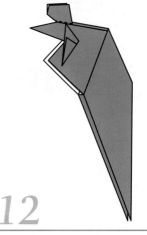

12

Outside reverse fold.

Buffalo

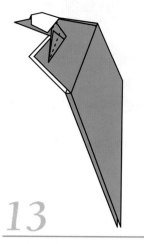

13

Valley folds, both sides.

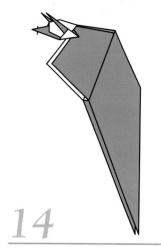

14

Outside reverse fold.

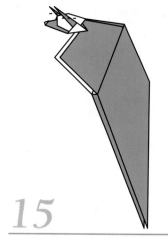

15

Valley folds.

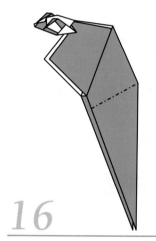

16

Inside reverse fold.

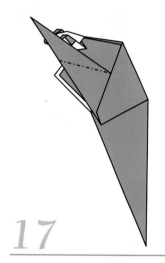

17

Inside reverse fold.

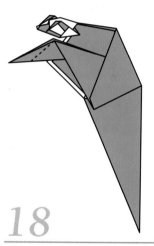

18

Outside reverse fold.

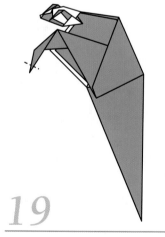

19

Inside reverse fold.

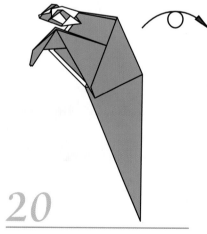

20

Turn over.

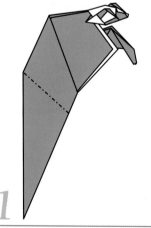

21

Inside reverse fold.

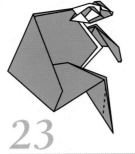
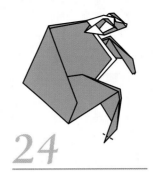

22
Inside reverse fold.

23
Outside reverse fold.

24
Inside reverse fold.

25
Completed part 1 (front) of buffalo.

Part 2

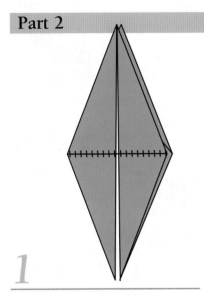
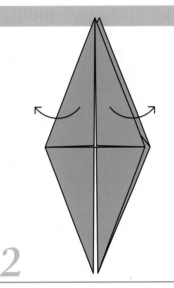
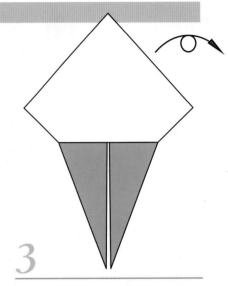

1
Start with Base Fold III. Cut as shown.

2
Valley unfolds.

3
Turn over.

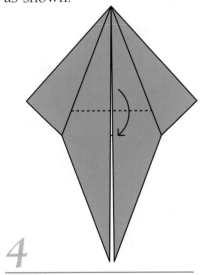
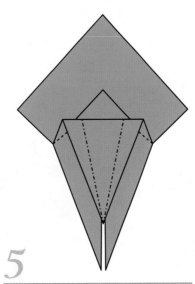
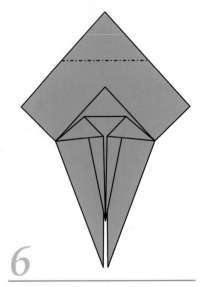

4
Valley fold.

5
Valley and squash folds.

6
Mountain fold.

Buffalo

41

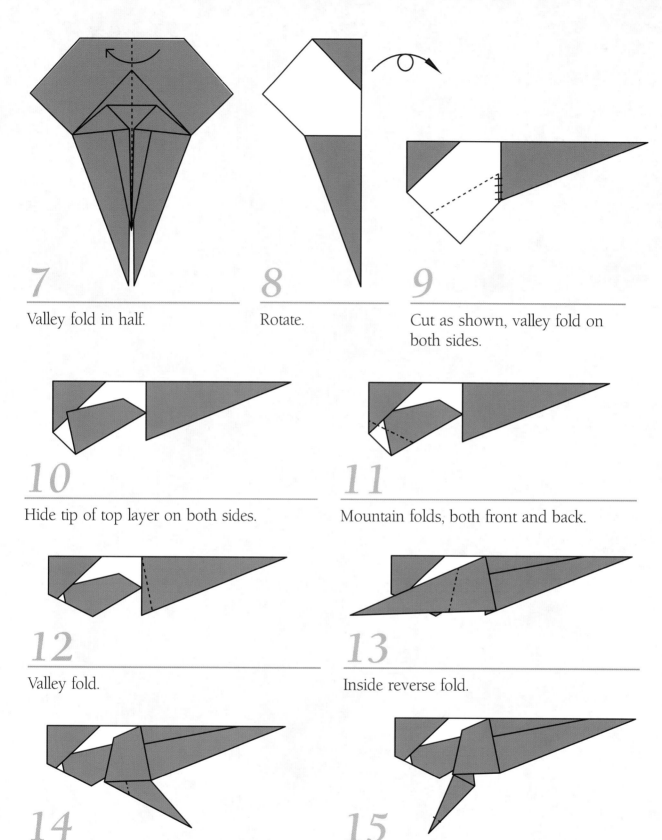

7

Valley fold in half.

8

Rotate.

9

Cut as shown, valley fold on both sides.

10

Hide tip of top layer on both sides.

11

Mountain folds, both front and back.

12

Valley fold.

13

Inside reverse fold.

14

Inside reverse fold.

15

Outside reverse fold.

Buffalo

42

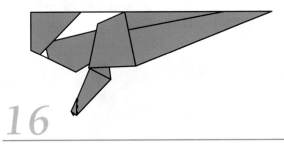

16

Inside reverse fold.

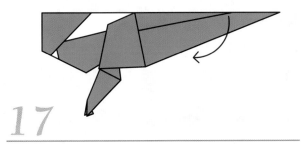

17

Pull in direction of arrow, squash fold into position.

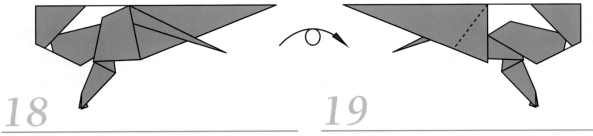

18

Turn over to other side.

19

Valley fold.

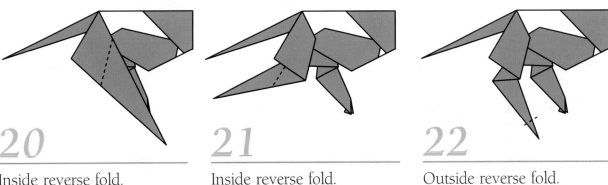

20

Inside reverse fold.

21

Inside reverse fold.

22

Outside reverse fold.

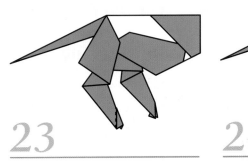

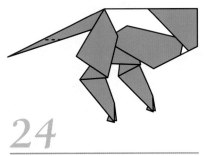

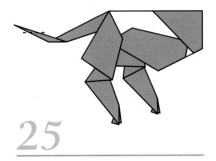

23

Inside reverse fold.

24

Outside reverse fold.

25

Outside reverse fold.

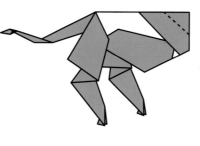

26
Squash fold in direction of arrow.

27
Inside reverse fold.

28
Completed part 2 (rear) of buffalo.

To Attach

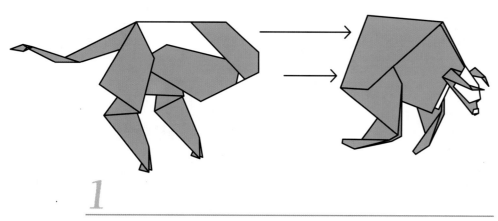

1
Join both parts together as shown and apply glue to hold.

2
Make cuts as shown.

Buffalo

3

Completed Buffalo.

George Washington

Part 1

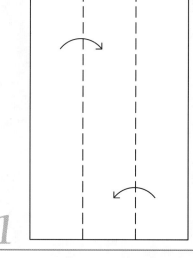

1 Valley fold both sides.

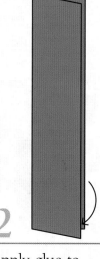

2 Apply glue to bottom only.

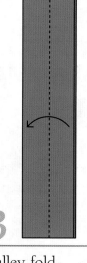

3 Valley fold.

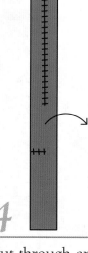

4 Cut through and valley unfold.

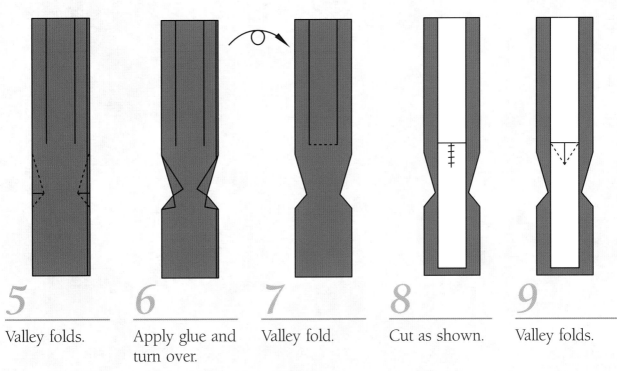

5	6	7	8	9
Valley folds.	Apply glue and turn over.	Valley fold.	Cut as shown.	Valley folds.

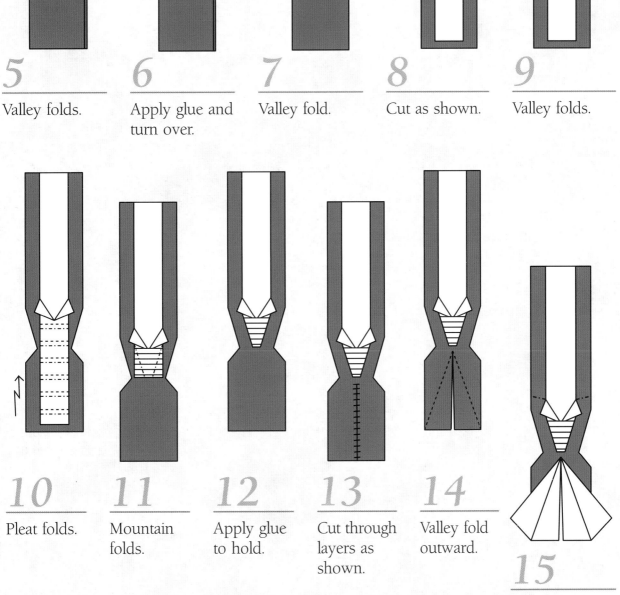

10	11	12	13	14
Pleat folds.	Mountain folds.	Apply glue to hold.	Cut through layers as shown.	Valley fold outward.

15

Mountain folds.

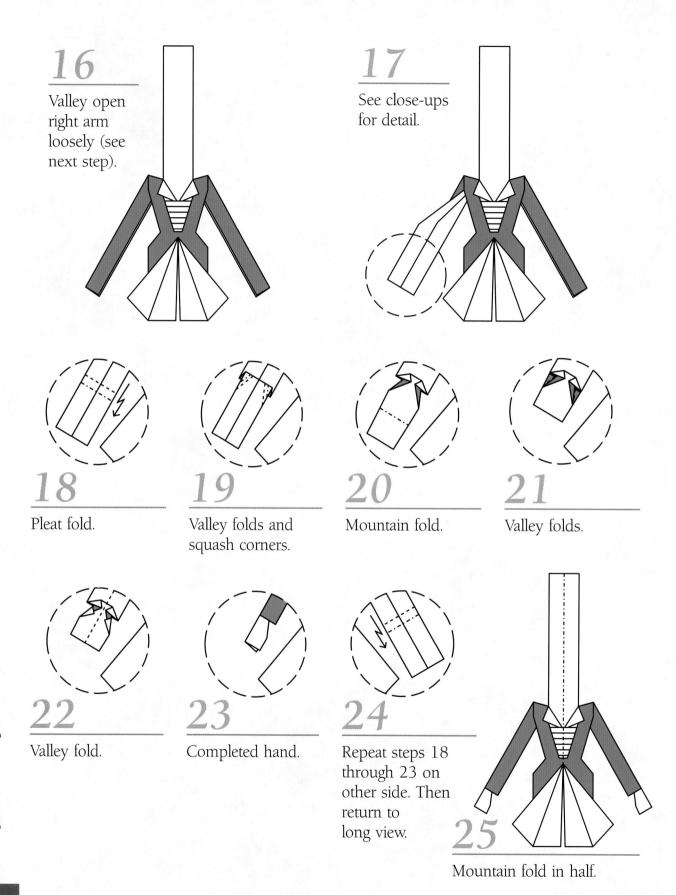

16
Valley open right arm loosely (see next step).

17
See close-ups for detail.

18
Pleat fold.

19
Valley folds and squash corners.

20
Mountain fold.

21
Valley folds.

22
Valley fold.

23
Completed hand.

24
Repeat steps 18 through 23 on other side. Then return to long view.

25
Mountain fold in half.

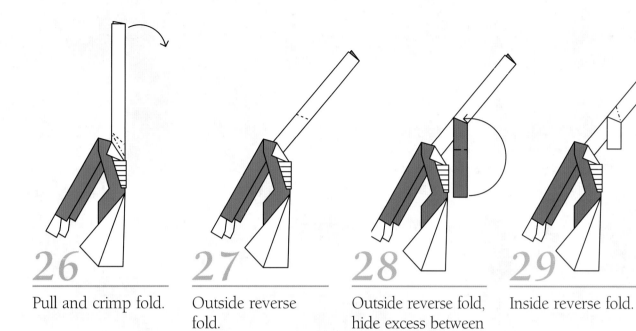

26

Pull and crimp fold.

27

Outside reverse fold.

28

Outside reverse fold, hide excess between layers.

29

Inside reverse fold.

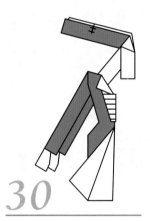

30

Cut as shown.

31

Valley folds.

32

Valley folds.

33

Outside reverse fold.

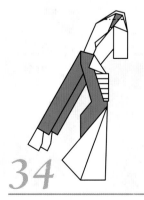

34

Mountain folds.

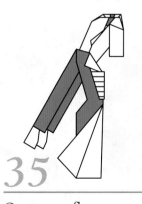

35

Open out flat.

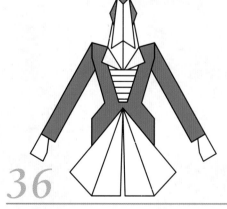

36

Completed part 1 (upper body) of George Washington.

Part 2 (standing position)

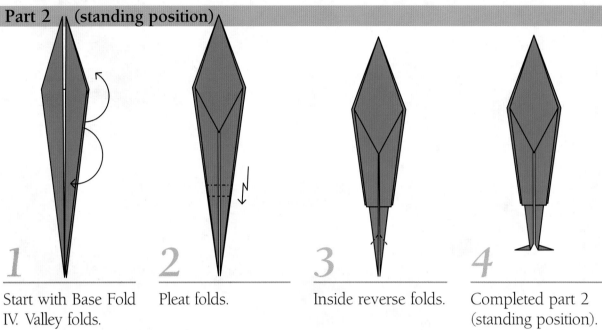

1 Start with Base Fold IV. Valley folds.

2 Pleat folds.

3 Inside reverse folds.

4 Completed part 2 (standing position).

Part 2 (astride position)

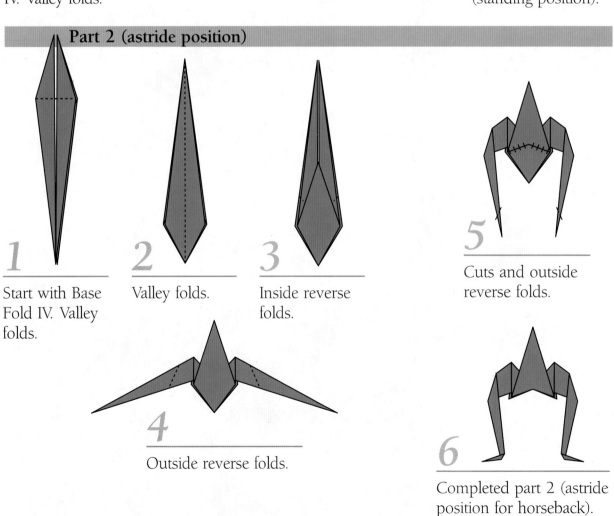

1 Start with Base Fold IV. Valley folds.

2 Valley folds.

3 Inside reverse folds.

4 Outside reverse folds.

5 Cuts and outside reverse folds.

6 Completed part 2 (astride position for horseback).

George Washington

Part 3 (hat)

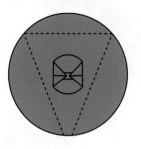

1

Make tri-cornered hat for George Washington (see Minuteman, page 66).

To Attach

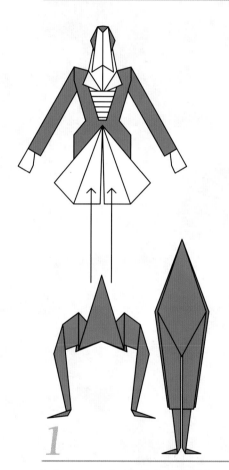

1

Join parts 1 and 2 (astride or standing) together and glue.

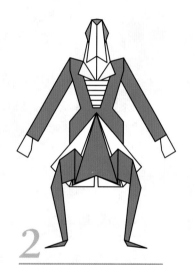

2

Mountain fold figure in half. Add coloring if wanted.

3

Add hat. If astride, fold arms for "riding." (Slit lower part of jacket up back, if needed, to fit on horse.)

4

Completed George Washington.

Washington's Horse

Part 1

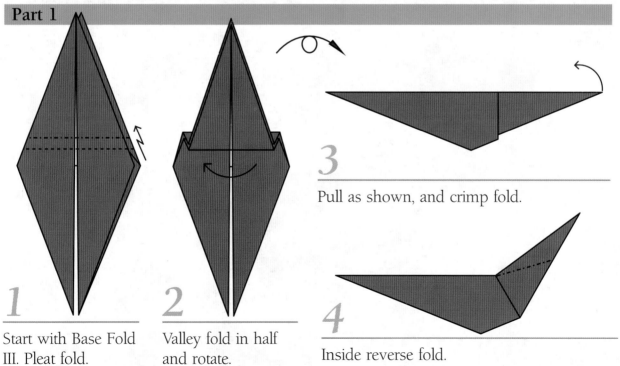

1
Start with Base Fold III. Pleat fold.

2
Valley fold in half and rotate.

3
Pull as shown, and crimp fold.

4
Inside reverse fold.

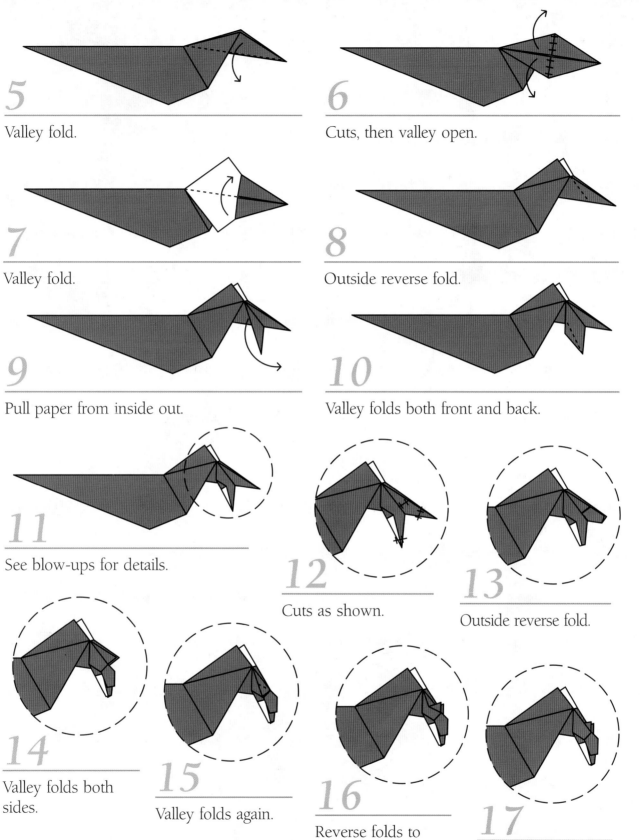

5
Valley fold.

6
Cuts, then valley open.

7
Valley fold.

8
Outside reverse fold.

9
Pull paper from inside out.

10
Valley folds both front and back.

11
See blow-ups for details.

12
Cuts as shown.

13
Outside reverse fold.

14
Valley folds both sides.

15
Valley folds again.

16
Reverse folds to tuck away flaps.

17
Return to full view.

Washington's Horse

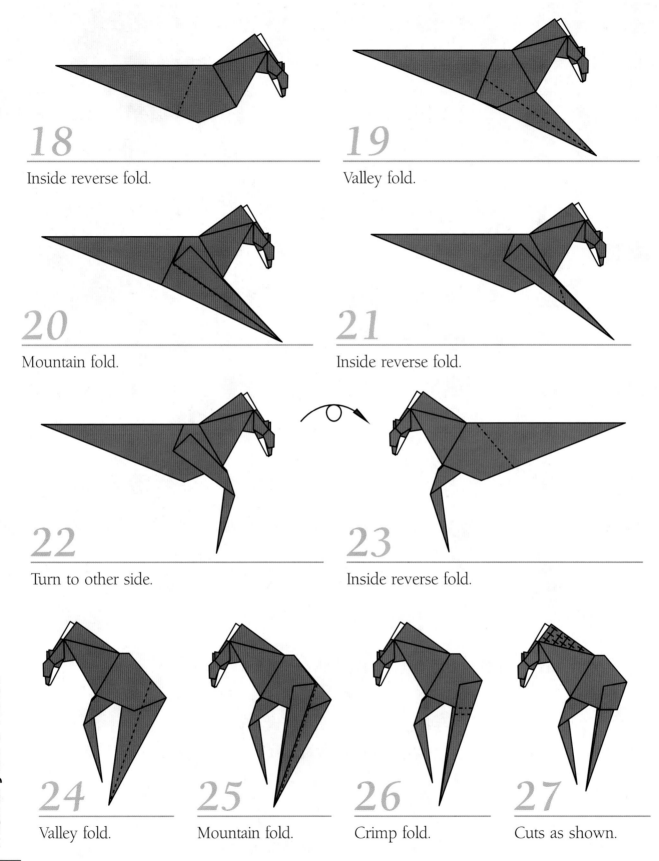

18

Inside reverse fold.

19

Valley fold.

20

Mountain fold.

21

Inside reverse fold.

22

Turn to other side.

23

Inside reverse fold.

24

Valley fold.

25

Mountain fold.

26

Crimp fold.

27

Cuts as shown.

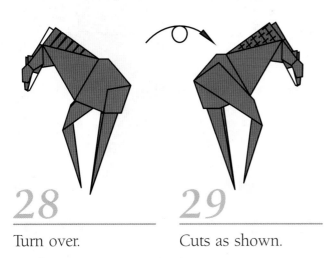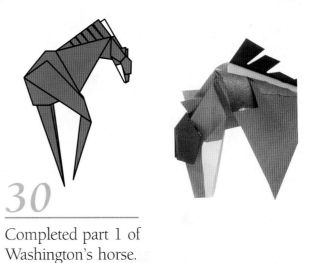

28

Turn over.

29

Cuts as shown.

30

Completed part 1 of Washington's horse.

Part 2

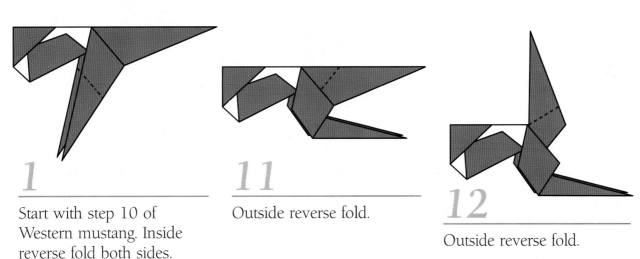

1

Start with step 10 of Western mustang. Inside reverse fold both sides.

11

Outside reverse fold.

12

Outside reverse fold.

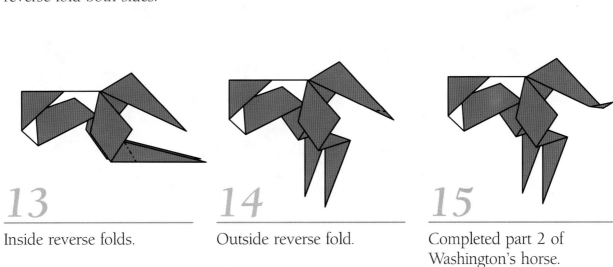

13

Inside reverse folds.

14

Outside reverse fold.

15

Completed part 2 of Washington's horse.

Washington's Horse

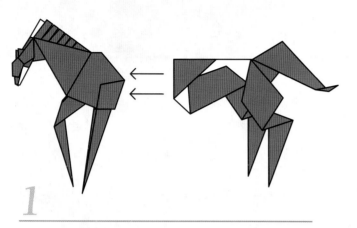

1

Join both parts together as shown and apply glue to hold.

2

Valley fold mane to side, and add coloring.

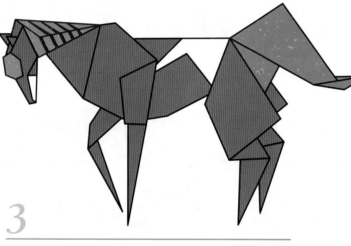

3

Completed Washington's Horse.

4

Place George Washington atop his horse, and apply glue to hold.

5

Add thin strips of paper for bridle and reins.

6

George Washington on his horse.

Betsy Ross

Part 1

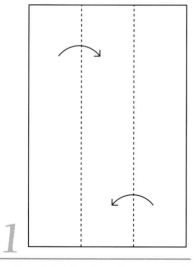

1   Valley fold both sides inward.

2   Apply glue at bottom only.

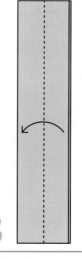

3   Valley fold.

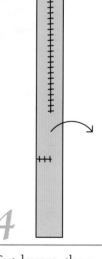

4   Cut layers, then open out.

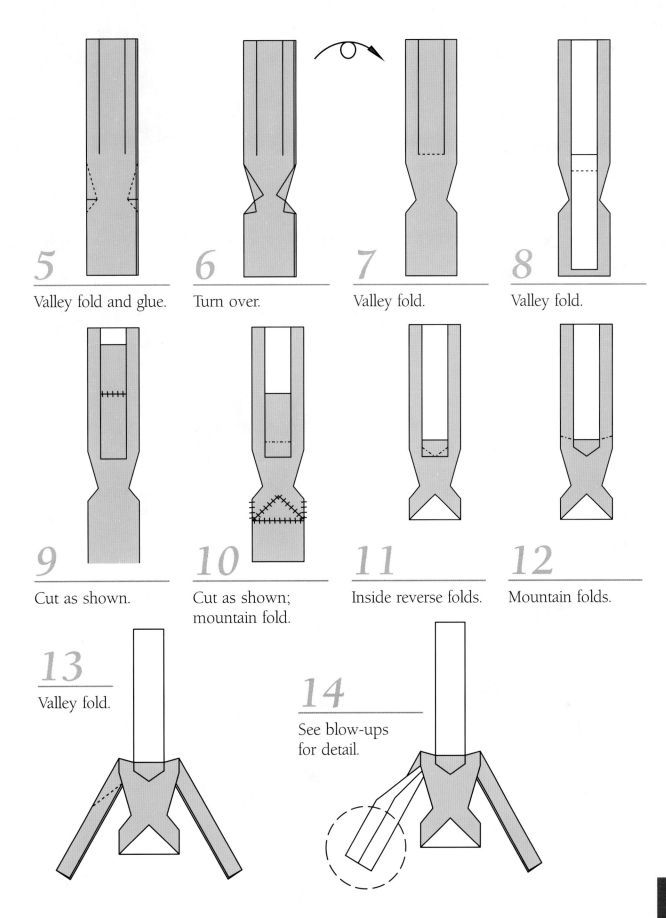

5
Valley fold and glue.

6
Turn over.

7
Valley fold.

8
Valley fold.

9
Cut as shown.

10
Cut as shown;
mountain fold.

11
Inside reverse folds.

12
Mountain folds.

13
Valley fold.

14
See blow-ups
for detail.

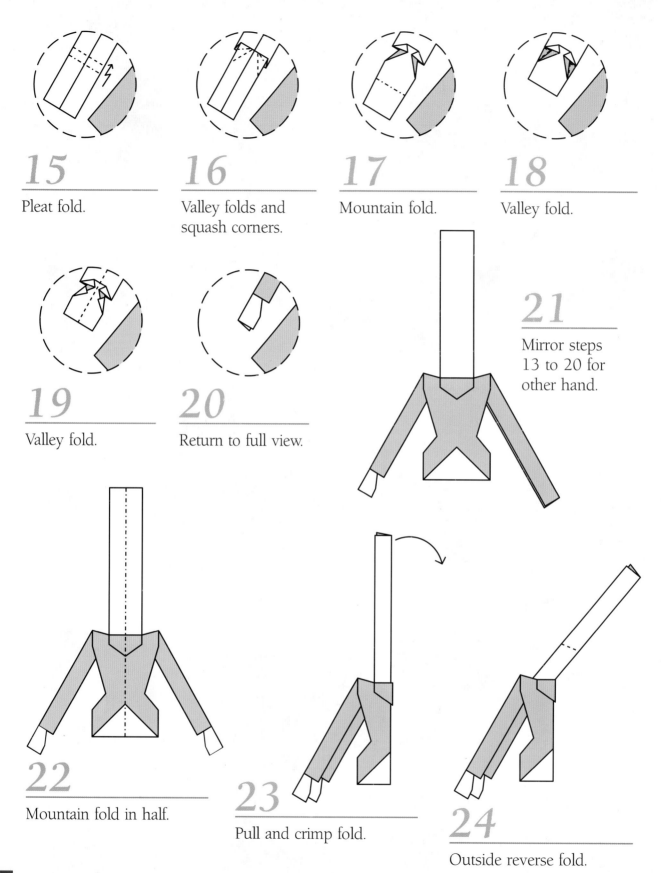

15

Pleat fold.

16

Valley folds and squash corners.

17

Mountain fold.

18

Valley fold.

19

Valley fold.

20

Return to full view.

21

Mirror steps 13 to 20 for other hand.

22

Mountain fold in half.

23

Pull and crimp fold.

24

Outside reverse fold.

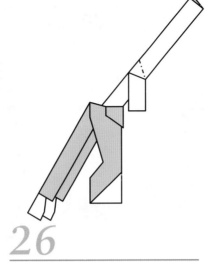

25

Outside reverse fold; slip excess inside.

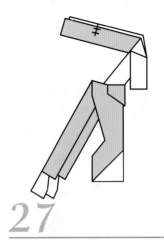

26

Inside reverse fold.

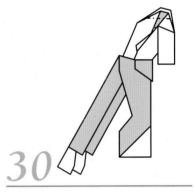

27

Cut as shown.

28

Valley folds.

29

Outside reverse fold.

30

Mountain folds.

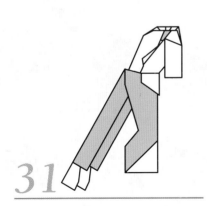

31

Open out figure.

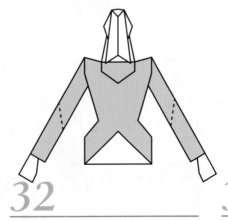

32

Valley folds.

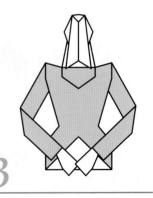

33

Completed part 1 (upper body) of Betsy Ross.

Part 2

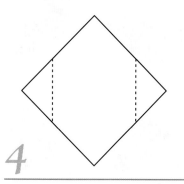

1
Roll into cone shape and glue to hold.

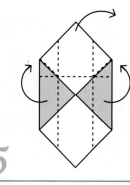

2
Cut as shown.

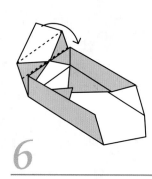

3
Completed part 2 (lower body) of Betsy Ross.

Part 3 (hat)

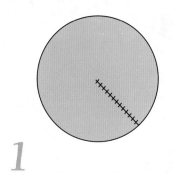

1
Cut paper circle as shown.

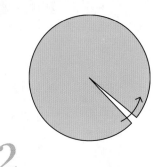

2
Pull and apply glue to hold.

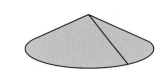

3
Completed brim.

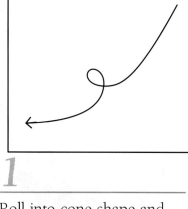

4
On square sheet, valley folds.

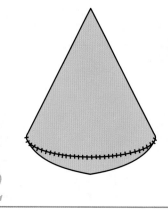

5
Valley fold sides upward to stand at 90 degrees.

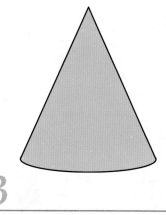

6
Valley fold and tuck flap into box-like shape.

Betsy Ross

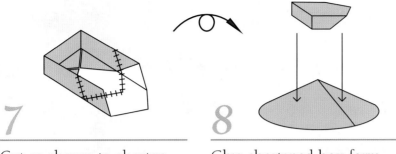

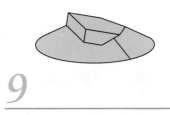

7

Cut as shown to shorten form, turn over.

8

Glue shortened box form to brim.

9

Completed Betsy Ross's hat.

To Attach

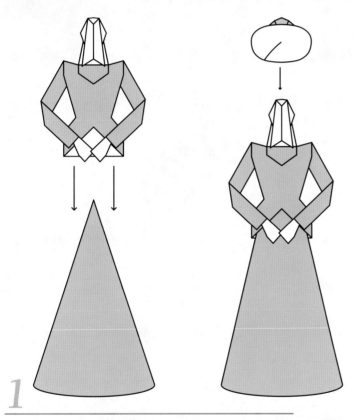

1

Join parts together as shown, apply glue to hold. If wanted, add color to face, hands, hair, inner hat; American flag suggested.

2

Completed Betsy Ross.

Minuteman

Parts 1 and 2

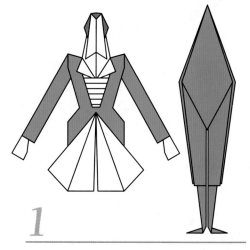

1

Use parts 1 (upper body) and 2 (lower body, standing) of George Washington (pages 46–50).

Part 3 (rifle)

1

Valley fold a length of dark paper in half.

2

Valley fold a second sheet to center.

3

Valley fold sides to center sides again, and then in half.

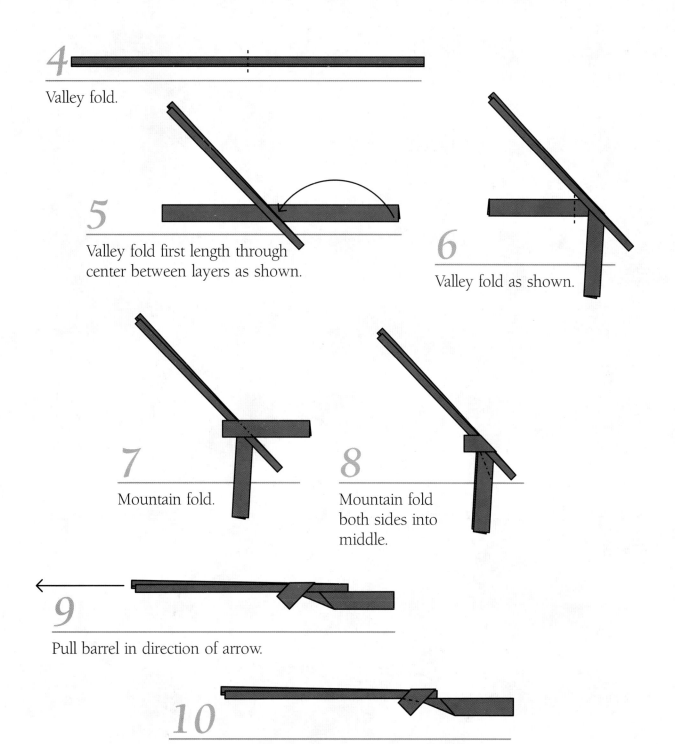

4

Valley fold.

5

Valley fold first length through center between layers as shown.

6

Valley fold as shown.

7

Mountain fold.

8

Mountain fold both sides into middle.

9

Pull barrel in direction of arrow.

10

Valley fold and apply glue to hold.

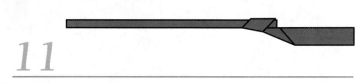

11

Completed part 3 (pioneer rifle).

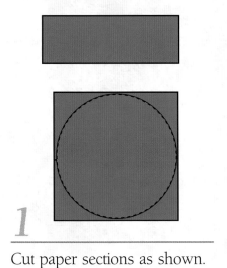

1
Cut paper sections as shown.

2
Roll rectangular length into a tube.

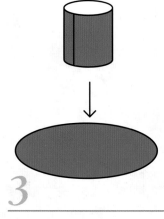

3
Join and apply glue to hold.

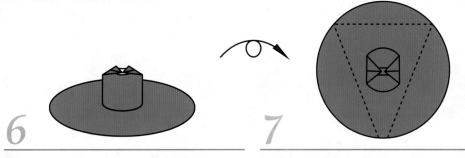

4
Mountain fold opposite sides inward to touch. Rotate.

5
Repeat mountain folds inward.

6
Rotate.

7
Valley fold brim upward at angles, as shown.

Overhead View

8
Completed tri-cornered hat.

Front View

1

Join parts 1 (upper body) and 2 (lower body) as shown. Apply glue to hold.

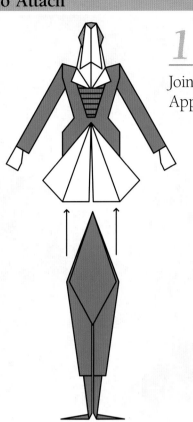

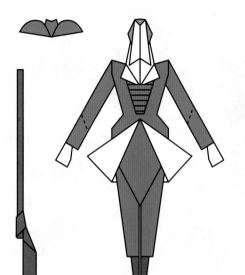

2

Position and valley fold arms to hold rifle. Add hat, and glue all to secure.

3

Completed Minuteman.

Minuteman

Pioneer Girl

Part 1

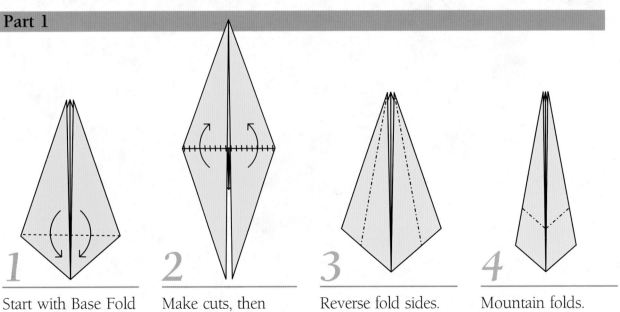

1 Start with Base Fold II; valley folds.

2 Make cuts, then valley fold back.

3 Reverse fold sides.

4 Mountain folds.

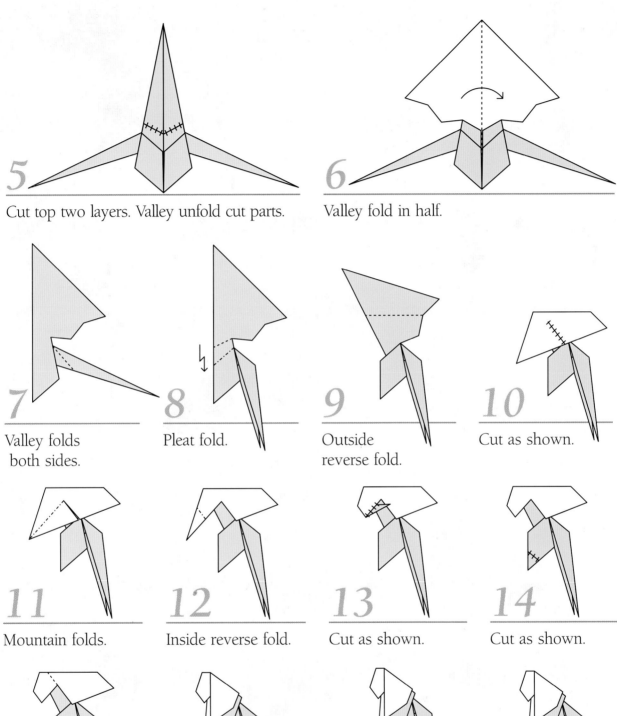

5
Cut top two layers. Valley unfold cut parts.

6
Valley fold in half.

7
Valley folds both sides.

8
Pleat fold.

9
Outside reverse fold.

10
Cut as shown.

11
Mountain folds.

12
Inside reverse fold.

13
Cut as shown.

14
Cut as shown.

15
Valley fold both sides.

16
Mountain folds.

17
Repeat.

18
Completed part 1 of pioneer girl.

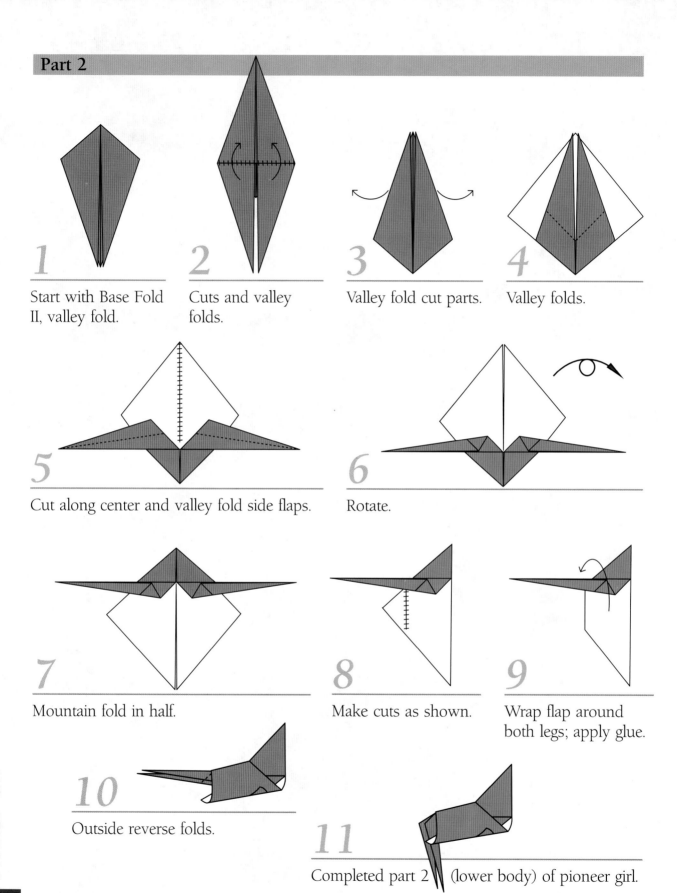

Part 2

1 Start with Base Fold II, valley fold.

2 Cuts and valley folds.

3 Valley fold cut parts.

4 Valley folds.

5 Cut along center and valley fold side flaps.

6 Rotate.

7 Mountain fold in half.

8 Make cuts as shown.

9 Wrap flap around both legs; apply glue.

10 Outside reverse folds.

11 Completed part 2 (lower body) of pioneer girl.

Part 3 (hat)

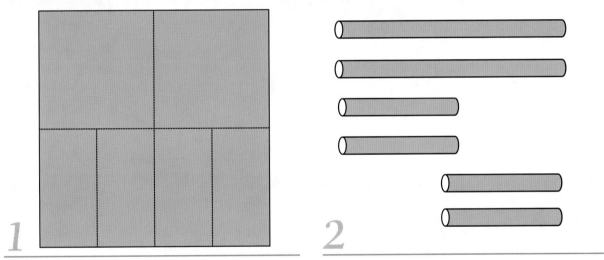

1

Make Betsy Ross hat (pages 64-65) for pioneer girl.

Part 4 (fence)

1

Cut large square apart; roll into tubes.

2

Completed log lengths.

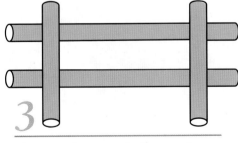

3

Position long and shorter logs as shown, and glue.

4

Place two remaining short logs into opening; and apply glue to attach.

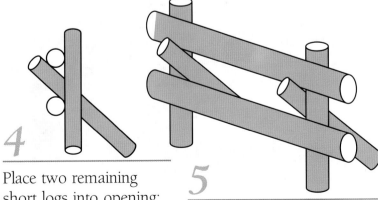

5

Completed part 4 (fence).

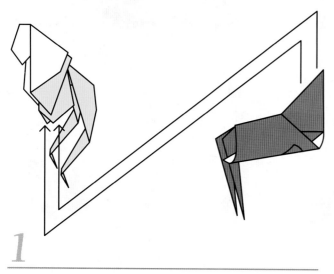

1

Add coloring to pioneer girl (shirt, hair) before joining body parts (1 and 2) together.

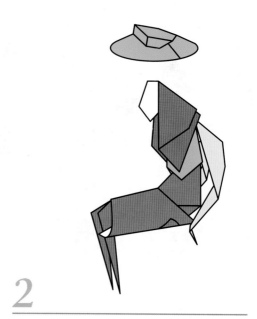

2

Add hat; apply glue to hold.

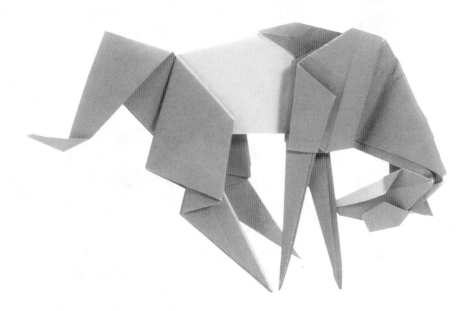

3

Position sitting pioneer girl on fence, and glue to hold.

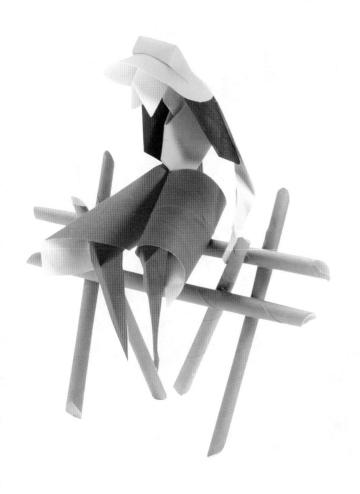

4

Completed Pioneer Girl.

Gunslinger

Part 1

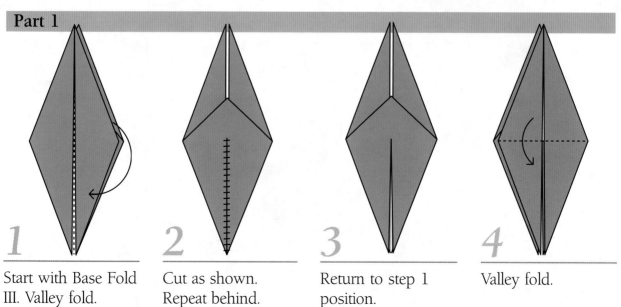

1
Start with Base Fold III. Valley fold.

2
Cut as shown. Repeat behind.

3
Return to step 1 position.

4
Valley fold.

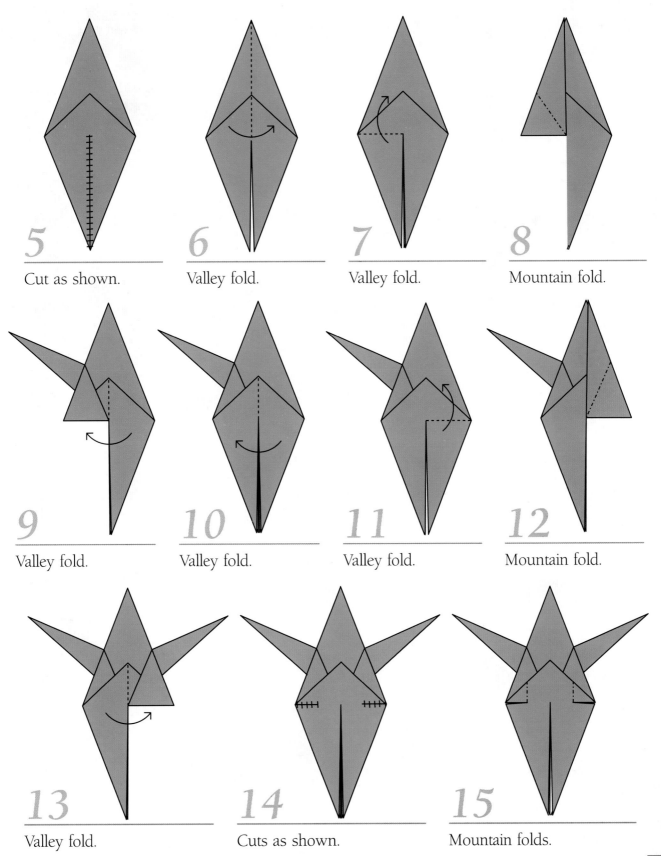

5

Cut as shown.

6

Valley fold.

7

Valley fold.

8

Mountain fold.

9

Valley fold.

10

Valley fold.

11

Valley fold.

12

Mountain fold.

13

Valley fold.

14

Cuts as shown.

15

Mountain folds.

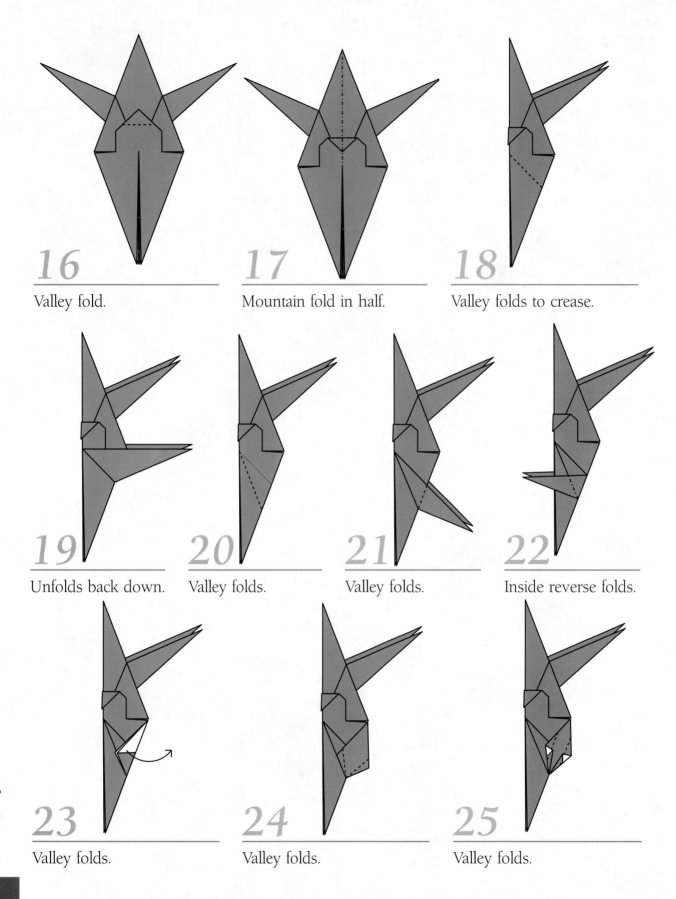

16
Valley fold.

17
Mountain fold in half.

18
Valley folds to crease.

19
Unfolds back down.

20
Valley folds.

21
Valley folds.

22
Inside reverse folds.

23
Valley folds.

24
Valley folds.

25
Valley folds.

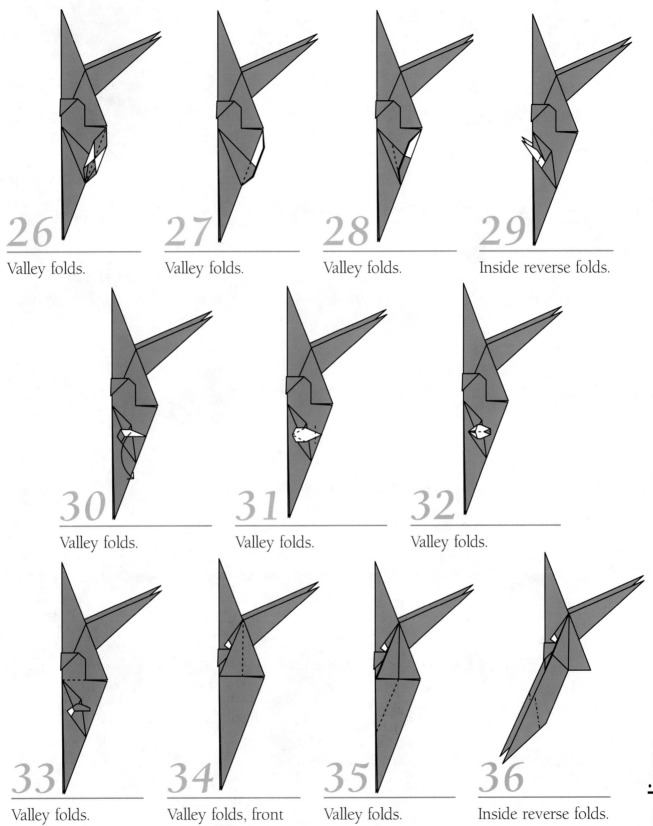

26
Valley folds.

27
Valley folds.

28
Valley folds.

29
Inside reverse folds.

30
Valley folds.

31
Valley folds.

32
Valley folds.

33
Valley folds.

34
Valley folds, front and back.

35
Valley folds.

36
Inside reverse folds.

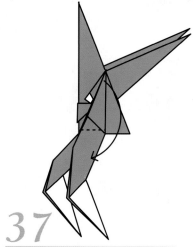

37
Valley folds both sides;
glue down.

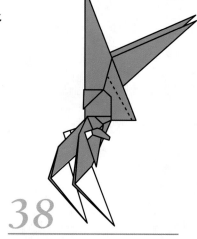

38
Valley folds.

39
Crimp fold.

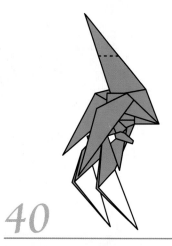

40
Outside reverse as shown.

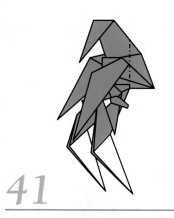

41
Mountain folds.

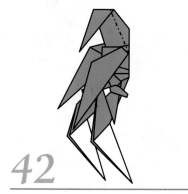

42
Repeat.

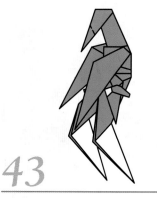

43
Inside reverse.

44
Cut as shown.

45

Valley folds.

46

Glue arm lengths to secure.

47

Valley folds.

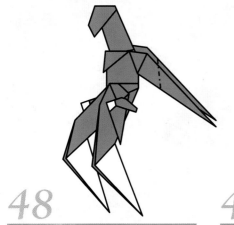

48

Mountain folds, both sides.

49

Inside reverse folds.

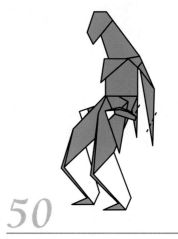

50

Valley folds.

51

Cuts as shown.

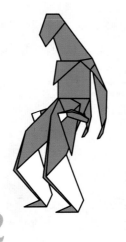

52

To complete, add coloring to figure as you wish.

53

Completed gunslinger (though hatless).

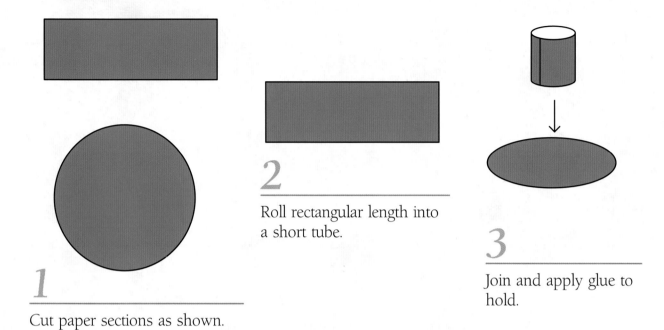

1

Cut paper sections as shown.

2

Roll rectangular length into a short tube.

3

Join and apply glue to hold.

4

Cut long strip as band, then trim ends to angle as shown.

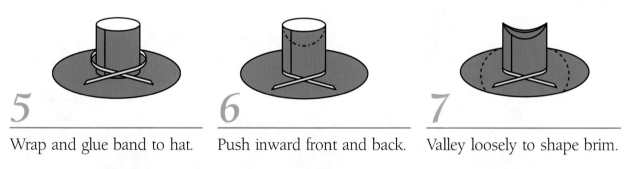

5

Wrap and glue band to hat.

6

Push inward front and back.

7

Valley loosely to shape brim.

8

Completed gunslinger's hat.

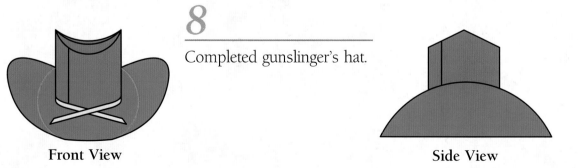

Front View

Side View

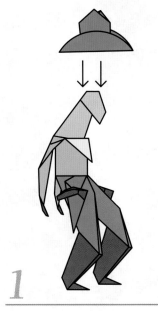

1

Place hat on head and
apply glue to hold.

2

Completed Gunslinger (front and side views).

Abraham Lincoln

Part 1

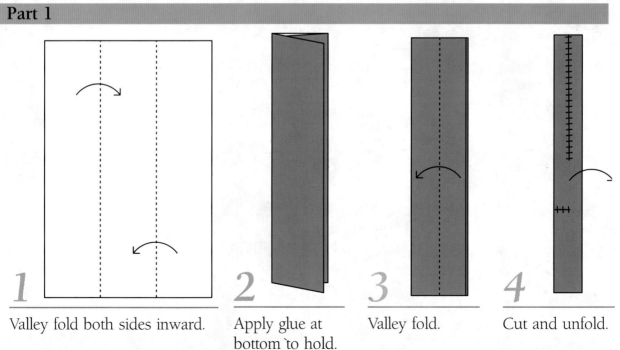

1 Valley fold both sides inward.

2 Apply glue at bottom to hold.

3 Valley fold.

4 Cut and unfold.

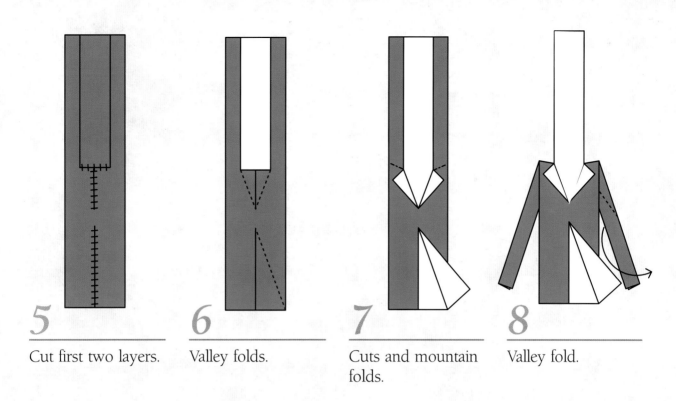

5
Cut first two layers.

6
Valley folds.

7
Cuts and mountain folds.

8
Valley fold.

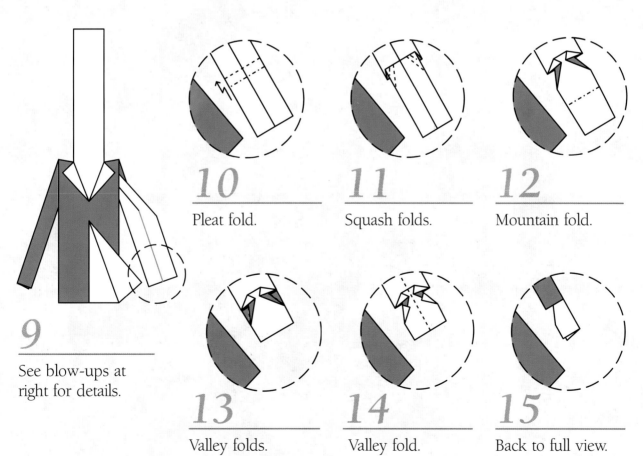

9
See blow-ups at right for details.

10
Pleat fold.

11
Squash folds.

12
Mountain fold.

13
Valley folds.

14
Valley fold.

15
Back to full view.

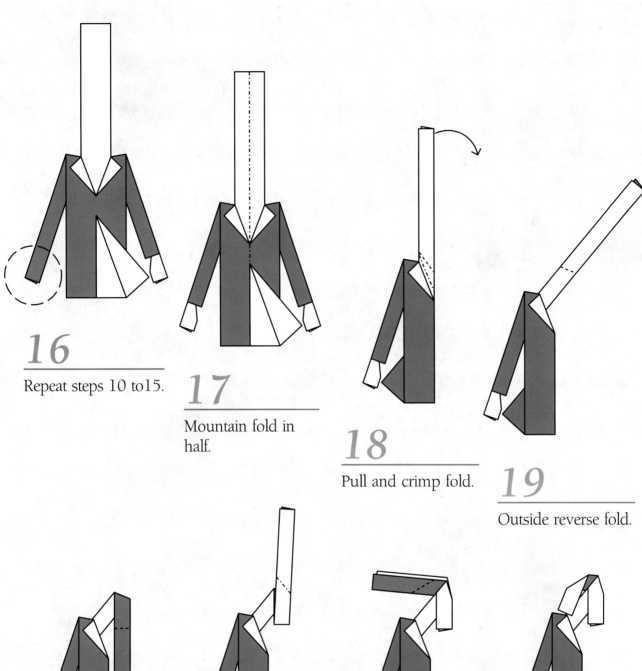

16
Repeat steps 10 to15.

17
Mountain fold in half.

18
Pull and crimp fold.

19
Outside reverse fold.

20
Repeat outside reverse.

21
Inside reverse fold.

22
Outside reverse fold.

23
Tuck between layers.

Abraham Lincoln

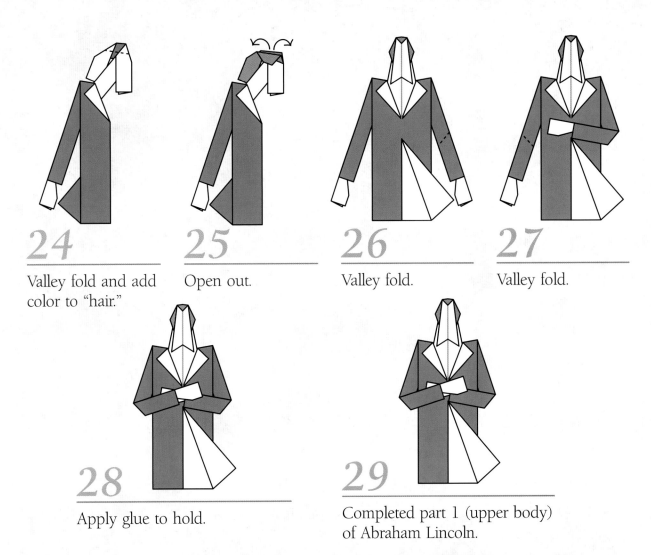

24
Valley fold and add color to "hair."

25
Open out.

26
Valley fold.

27
Valley fold.

28
Apply glue to hold.

29
Completed part 1 (upper body) of Abraham Lincoln.

Part 2

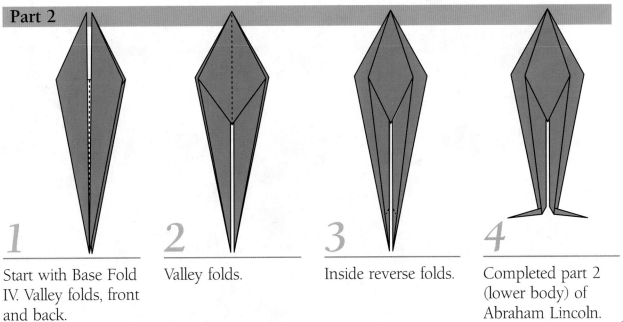

1
Start with Base Fold IV. Valley folds, front and back.

2
Valley folds.

3
Inside reverse folds.

4
Completed part 2 (lower body) of Abraham Lincoln.

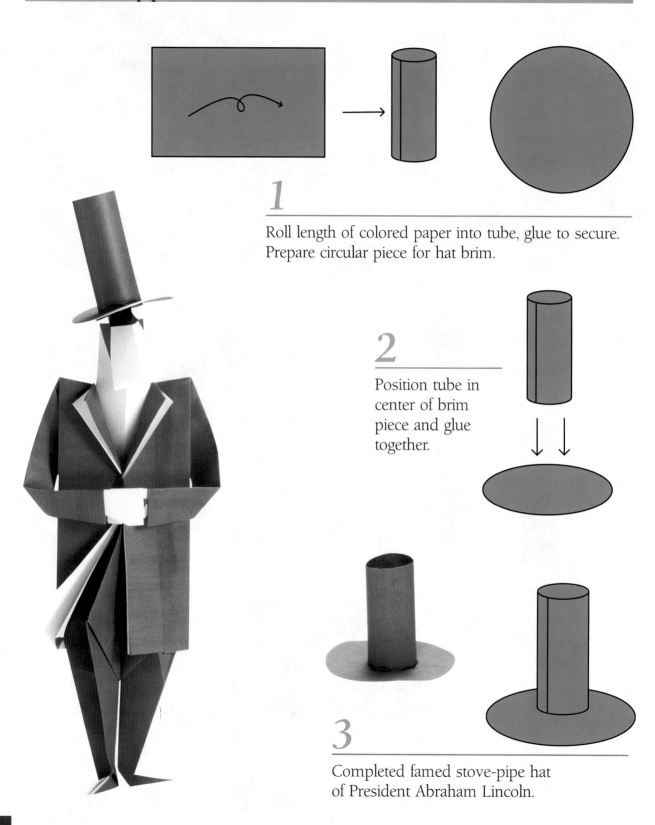

1

Roll length of colored paper into tube, glue to secure. Prepare circular piece for hat brim.

2

Position tube in center of brim piece and glue together.

3

Completed famed stove-pipe hat of President Abraham Lincoln.

Abraham Lincoln

1

Join parts 1 and 2 (upper and lower body) of Abraham Lincoln together as shown, and apply glue to hold.

2

Add stove-pipe hat.

3

Completed Abraham Lincoln.

The King: Elvis

Part 1

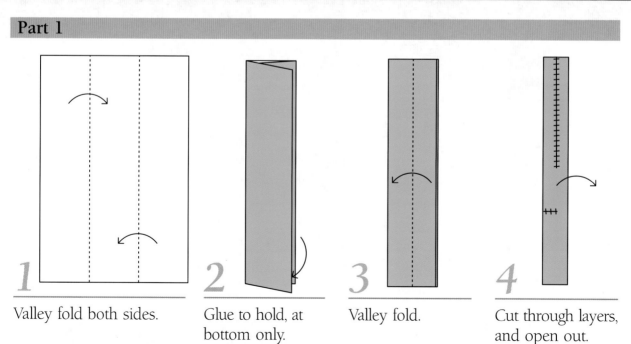

1 Valley fold both sides.

2 Glue to hold, at bottom only.

3 Valley fold.

4 Cut through layers, and open out.

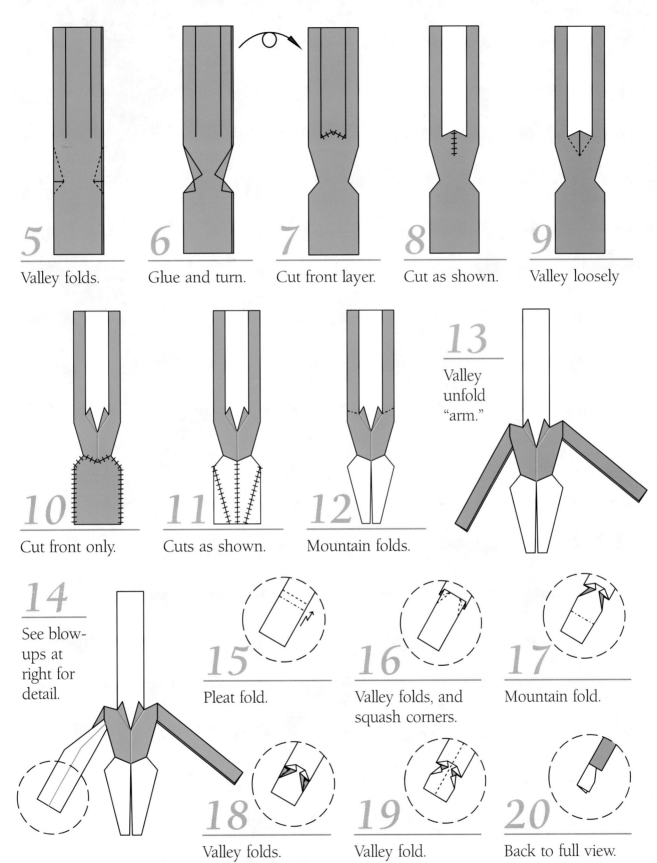

5 Valley folds.

6 Glue and turn.

7 Cut front layer.

8 Cut as shown.

9 Valley loosely

10 Cut front only.

11 Cuts as shown.

12 Mountain folds.

13 Valley unfold "arm."

14 See blow-ups at right for detail.

15 Pleat fold.

16 Valley folds, and squash corners.

17 Mountain fold.

18 Valley folds.

19 Valley fold.

20 Back to full view.

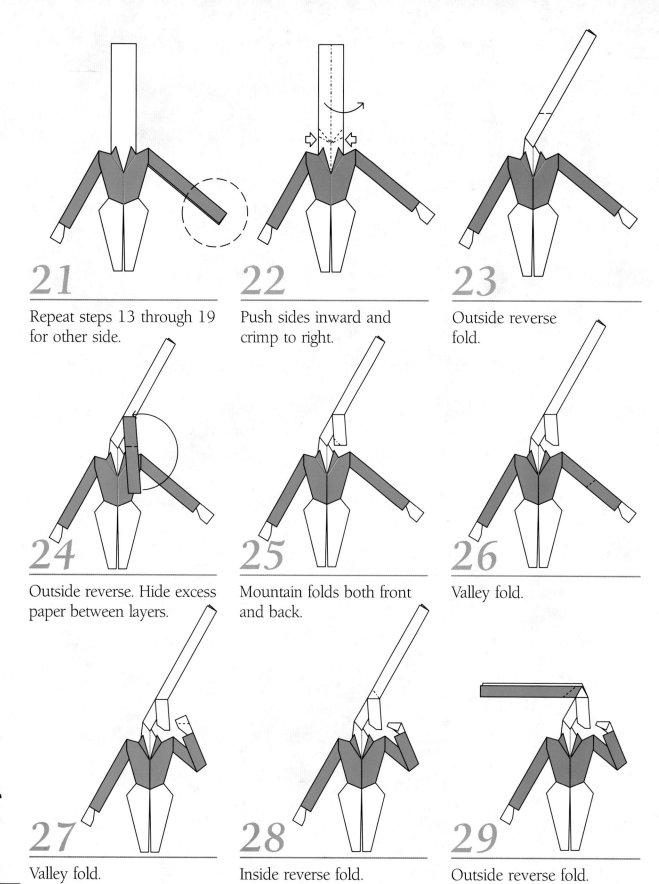

21

Repeat steps 13 through 19 for other side.

22

Push sides inward and crimp to right.

23

Outside reverse fold.

24

Outside reverse. Hide excess paper between layers.

25

Mountain folds both front and back.

26

Valley fold.

27

Valley fold.

28

Inside reverse fold.

29

Outside reverse fold.

30
Outside reverse fold.

31
Inside reverse fold.

32
Inside reverse fold.

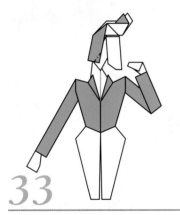

33
Mountain folds.

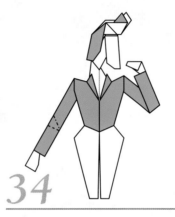

34
Crimp fold.

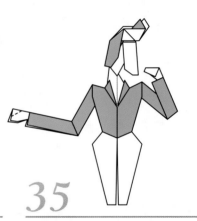

35
Valley fold.

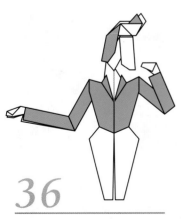

36
Add coloring to figure.

37
Completed part 1
(upper body) of The King.

Part 2

1

Start with rectangular sheet--
about 4 by 11 inches (12 by
28 cm) if you used 8 or 8½-
inch squares for body. Crease
down center, then valley fold
sides into center as shown,
and valley fold in half.

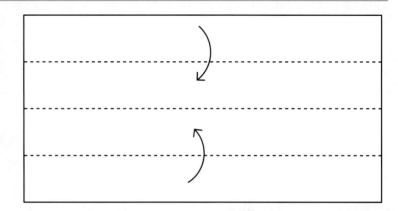

2

Valley fold in half, then outside reverse folds.

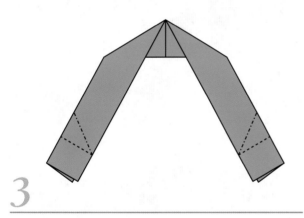

3

Crimp fold both sides.

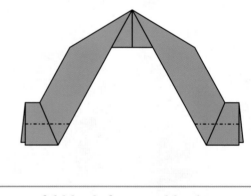

4

Mountain fold both front and back.

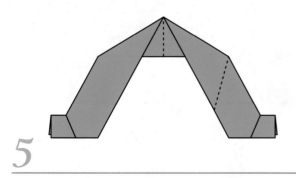

5

Valley folds, then apply color.

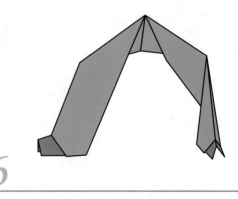

6

Completed part 2 (legs) of The King.

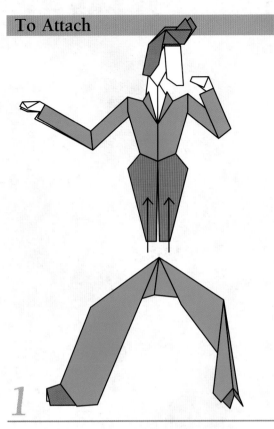

1

Join both parts together as shown, apply glue to hold.

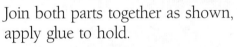

2

Add a small roll of paper (to serve as microphone) and glue.

3

The King! Completed Elvis.

The King: Elvis

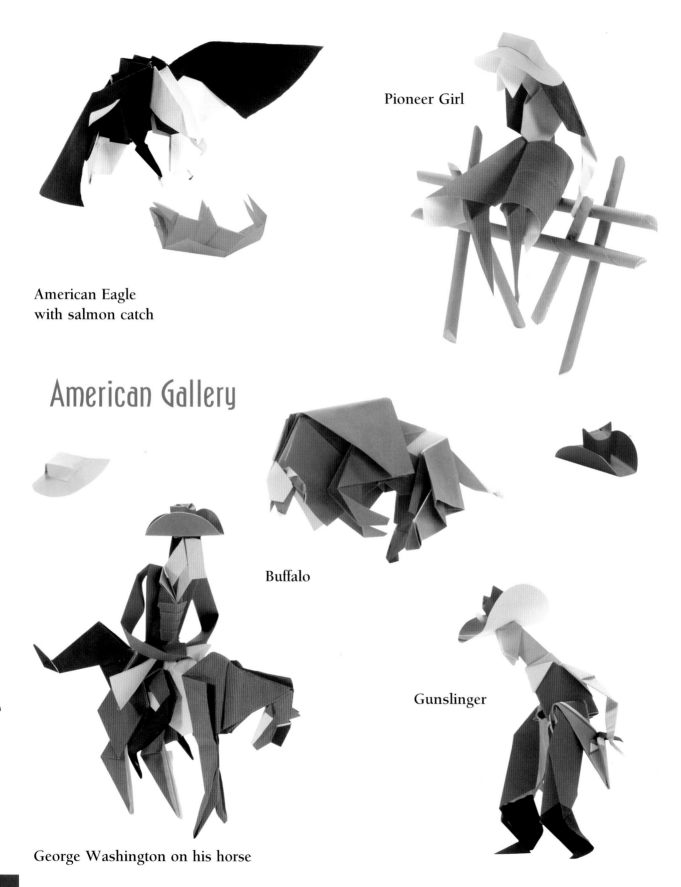

Pioneer Girl

American Eagle
with salmon catch

American Gallery

Buffalo

Gunslinger

George Washington on his horse

The King: Elvis

Betsy Ross

Minuteman

Native American
on Mustang

Abraham Lincoln

American Gallery

95

Index